# 2011

### A Book of
### Grace-Filled
### Days

M A R G A R E T    S I L F

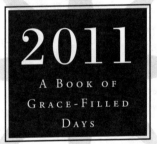

# 2011

## A BOOK OF
## GRACE-FILLED
## DAYS

LOYOLA PRESS.
A JESUIT MINISTRY
Chicago

# LOYOLA PRESS.
## A JESUIT MINISTRY

3441 N. Ashland Avenue
Chicago, Illinois 60657
(800) 621-1008
www.loyolapress.com

*Cover and interior design by Kathy Kikkert*

**Library of Congress Cataloging-in-Publication Data**
Silf, Margaret.
  2011 : a book of grace-filled days / Margaret Silf.
    p. cm.
  ISBN-13: 978-0-8294-2911-4
  ISBN-10: 0-8294-2911-5
  1. Devotional calendars—Catholic Church. 2. Catholic Church—Prayers and devotions. I. Title. II. Title: Twenty eleven.
  BX2170.C56S56 2011
  242'.2—dc22

                                             2010010504

Printed in the United States of America
10  11  12  13  14  15  Bang  10  9  8  7  6  5  4  3  2  1

# INTRODUCTION

This series of daily reflections began during Lent, some fifteen years ago, in a small parish in an industrial area of the northwestern Midlands of England. The people of that parish were looking for ways to deepen their spiritual life, and they asked me to write a few reflections on the lectionary readings for the weeks leading up to Easter. These reflections appeared as a series of weekly leaflets available to anyone who wanted to take one. I called them "Potter's Clay" because the parish was in that part of England that is home to the ceramics industry and is commonly called the Potteries.

I could not have guessed then that this small and very local Lenten journey would continue not just beyond Easter but also through many years to come—and that it would cross the Atlantic in 2001 to appear under the title *A Book of Grace-Filled Days*. I am delighted to be able to rejoin the book's journey now, on the tenth anniversary of its first beginnings in the United States.

There is an ancient practice of scriptural meditation known as *lectio divina*. In the past, when very few people could read, it was common for monks to gather for morning meditation and simply listen in prayerful silence, as one among them who was able to do so would read the Scripture for the day. That monk would read slowly and reflectively while the others listened, and whenever each of them felt that a particular word or phrase or image was especially potent for him that day, he would leave the chapel and go to his cell to meditate on whatever had captured his imagination. He would chew it over in his heart and in his mind until he felt he had found what it was that God was saying to him that morning through what he had heard. The process could be compared to sucking on a sweet until all the flavor has been extracted. The reader would continue to keep reading and rereading the Scriptures until there was no one left in the chapel.

Today we live in a very different world from that of these ancient monks, but *lectio divina* is still a very powerful form of scriptural prayer and is practiced by many Christians on a regular basis. It is the way *A Book of Grace-Filled Days* has been written. I begin by reading the daily texts from the lectionary and simply noticing what in particular seems to spring to life for me as I do so. That nugget then becomes the basis for my reflection.

Sometimes the readings seem to draw me to reflect on things that are happening in my own life or in the wider world. Sometimes they open up new ways of "finding God in all things"—as St. Ignatius of Loyola would say—in the daily journey of life. Always they lead more deeply into the sacred texts. And the strange and wonderful thing is that when we seek to get inside Scripture in this or any other way, what actually happens is the opposite. It is Scripture that gets inside *us*, shaping us, forming us, challenging us, and sometimes flattening us and beginning all over again to re-create us—a bit like clay on the potter's wheel.

Most of us don't begin our days in chapel listening to the lectionary readings but in the tumult of family life, in the challenges of the workplace, or in the loneliness of an empty room far from our loved ones. Nor do we continue our reflections in a quiet monastic cell but on the highway, in the classroom, on the factory floor, or on the streets. None of this should prevent us from adapting the process of *lectio divina* to our twenty-first-century lives. If you take an extract from the daily readings as the starting point for your prayer each day, notice what seems to speak to you especially, and keep bringing that phrase or image or thought to mind as you go through your day whenever you have a moment—perhaps during your coffee break, in the shower, in traffic—then you are practicing *lectio divina*.

I hope that this year's reflections will help you make your own journey of scriptural meditation as the days go by. Perhaps you are a seasoned traveler who has journeyed with the series since its first inception. Perhaps this is your first introduction to the possibility of daily scriptural reflection. Either way, welcome to the journey of a year that can become the journey of a lifetime, and may every day of 2011 be full of grace.

# NOVEMBER 28

*So too, you also must be prepared, for at an hour you do not expect, the Son of Man will come.*

—MATTHEW 24:44

A recorded message: "Sorry I was out when you called. Please leave your name and number."

Will this be my response to the touch of God upon my life? To that totally unexpected moment when I know beyond doubt that God *is* and that God is in touch with *me*?

God doesn't leave messages; God speaks to the heart. May we keep our lines open 24/7.

Isaiah 2:1–5
Psalm 122
Romans 13:11–14
Matthew 24:37–44

*On that day,*
*The branch of the LORD will be luster and glory,*
*and the fruit of the earth will be honor and splendor*
*for the survivors of Israel.*

—ISAIAH 4:2

After the long winter months, the prophet Isaiah speaks of an amazing springtime. Then the trees of the forest that have withstood the frosts and gales will begin to reveal what they truly are. What will be the blossoms and fruits of human life on this planet? Dare we trust this promise that, in God's hands, the fruits will be beauty and glory, reflecting the image of the Creator, and that the darkest hours we experience are truly cultivating God's springtime?

Isaiah 4:2–6
Psalm 122
Matthew 8:5–11

*As Jesus was walking by the Sea of Galilee, he saw two brothers, Simon who is called Peter, and his brother Andrew, casting a net into the sea; they were fishermen. He said to them, "Come after me, and I will make you fishers of men." At once they left their nets and followed him.*
—MATTHEW 4:18–20

Jesus calls these men to become fishers of men because they are already fishers of fish. He calls them to move to a deeper engagement with the gifts and experience they already have. As always, he draws our attention to the real world and circumstances in which we live and work, and he shows us how those circumstances might reflect the glory of God, if we will only follow and trust. We are not all fishermen. What gifts and experience is Jesus calling forth in you? How will you respond?

Romans 10:9–18
Psalm 19
Matthew 4:18–22

# DECEMBER 1

*[Jesus] ordered the crowd to sit down on the ground. Then he took the seven loaves and the fish, gave thanks, broke the loaves, and gave them to the disciples, who in turn gave them to the crowds. They all ate and were satisfied. They picked up the fragments left over—seven baskets full.*

—MATTHEW 15:35–37

What we, in the affluent nations, waste might fill the tables of the poor seven times over, but it will take a miracle to make us see this and act upon it.

Isaiah 25:6–10
Psalm 23
Matthew 15:29–37

"*Not everyone who says to me, 'Lord, Lord,' will enter the kingdom of heaven, but only the one who does the will of my Father in heaven.*"

—MATTHEW 7:21

At a Quaker meeting a visitor breaks the silence to ask his neighbor, "When does the service begin?"

The reply: "As soon as the worship finishes."

Isaiah 26:1–6
Psalm 118
Matthew 7:21, 24–27

---

# DECEMBER 3

• ST. FRANCIS XAVIER, PRIEST •

*On that day the deaf shall hear*
*the words of a book;*
*And out of gloom and darkness,*
*the eyes of the blind shall see.*

—ISAIAH 29:18

When my ears are deafened by the clamor of the world's distractions, and my eyes are dazzled by its fleeting attractions, God's promise breaks through: "I will open the ears and the eyes of your heart."

Isaiah 29:17–24
Psalm 27
Matthew 9:27–31

# DECEMBER 4

• ST. JOHN OF DAMASCUS, PRIEST AND DOCTOR OF THE CHURCH •

*The light of the moon will be like that of the sun*
*and the light of the sun will be seven times greater*
*like the light of seven days.*
*On the day the LORD binds up the wounds of his people,*
*he will heal the bruises left by his blows.*

—ISAIAH 30:26

In the night of our fears and sorrows, we grope our way through life by the meager candlelight of our wavering faith. But slowly, gradually, those lights are leading us into a new dawn that will outshine them all.

Isaiah 30:19–21, 23–26
Psalm 147
Matthew 9:35—10:1, 5a, 6–8

*There shall be no harm or ruin on all my holy mountain;*
*for the earth shall be filled with knowledge of the LORD,*
*as water covers the sea.*

—ISAIAH 11:9

If I truly could know my enemies, I would understand them. If I truly could understand them, I would be able to forgive them. And if I can forgive them, I can no longer cause them harm. The tide of God's love will wash clean the messy shoreline of my heart.

Isaiah 11:1–10
Psalm 72
Romans 15:4–9
Matthew 3:1–12

---

# DECEMBER 6

*Kindness and truth shall meet;*
*justice and peace shall kiss.*
*Truth will spring out of the earth,*
*and justice shall look down from heaven.*

—PSALM 85:11–12

The coming of God's reign is not so much about obeying a command as it is about surrendering to an embrace. In that embrace, miracles happen.

Isaiah 35:1–10
Psalm 85
Luke 5:17–26

*A voice cries out:*
*In the desert prepare the way of the LORD!*
*Make straight in the wasteland a highway for our God!*

—ISAIAH 40:3

I have my own ideas about where God's highway should be routed in my life: it should take in all the best bits and my achievements and successes. God has other ideas. God's way leads right into and through my wilderness, my mess, my chaos and my failures.

Isaiah 40:1–11
Psalm 96
Matthew 18:12–14

⇒ 10 ⇐

*And the angel said to her in reply, "The Holy Spirit will come upon you, and the power of the Most High will overshadow you. Therefore the child to be born will be called holy, the Son of God."*

—LUKE 1:35

In God the inconceivable becomes a reality, but only if we are willing to allow our shallow ego-selves to be eclipsed by the overshadowing mystery of the Holy Spirit, in whose power all things are possible. May the grace of this Holy Spirit overshadow all our world's strivings, so that we might truly become the holy people God created us to be.

Genesis 3:9–15, 20
Psalm 98
Ephesians 1:3–6, 11–12
Luke 1:26–38

*I am the LORD, your God,*
*who grasp your right hand;*
*It is I who say to you, "Fear not,*
*I will help you."*

—ISAIAH 41:13

When I am floundering on the mountainside of life, I don't need a map or a guidebook. I need someone who takes me by the hand, guides me through the rocks and gullies, and gives me the courage to keep walking.

Isaiah 41:13–20
Psalm 145
Matthew 11:11–15

*Friday*

# DECEMBER 10

*Thus says the LORD, your redeemer,*
*the Holy One of Israel:*
*I, the LORD, your God,*
*teach you what is for your good,*
*and lead you on the way you should go.*

—ISAIAH 48:17

There will be many others who claim to lead us, and often they will wear the disguise of authority. May we have the grace of a discerning heart to know what is of God and what is not.

Isaiah 48:17–19
Psalm 1
Matthew 11:16–19

# DECEMBER 11

*I tell you that Elijah has already come, and they did not recognize him but did to him whatever they pleased. So also will the Son of Man suffer at their hands.*

—MATTHEW 17:12

The voice of prophecy is alive in the twenty-first century, warning us that God is present in the ones we mistreat.

Can we recognize it? Dare we hear it?

How will we respond?

Sirach 48:1–4, 9–11
Psalm 80
Matthew 17:9a, 10–13

*The LORD gives sight to the blind;*
*the LORD raises up those who are bowed down.*
*The LORD loves the just;*
*the LORD protects strangers.*
—PSALM 146:8–9

The teacher who helps a child solve a problem;
the teenager who stops to share a word and a sandwich
with a homeless person;
the activist who insists on justice for the asylum seeker;
the neighbor who looks out for the latchkey kids on the
block—
they are all reflecting the glory of the Lord.

Isaiah 35:1–6, 10
Psalm 146
James 5:7–10
Matthew 11:2–11

# DECEMBER 13

*I see him, though not now;*
*I behold him, though not near:*
*A star shall advance from Jacob,*
*and a staff shall rise from Israel.*

—NUMBERS 24:17

The writer and Nobel Prize winner André Gide reminds us that "ideals are like stars: we can never reach them, but we can use them to help us plot our course." The star from Jacob will be forever beyond our reach, yet it will dwell within us always, guiding our every step.

Numbers 24:2–7; 15–17
Psalm 25
Matthew 21:23–27

*I will leave as a remnant in your midst*
*a people humble and lowly,*
*Who shall take refuge in the name of the LORD.*

—ZEPHANIAH 3:12

Even when we feel that hardly anyone is left who knows or loves God, who reaches out to the suffering or speaks out for justice—even then, God is nurturing a core of faithfulness and love. Do we believe this? Will we look for it?

Zephaniah 3:1–2, 9–13
Psalm 34
Matthew 21:28–32

*Go and tell John what you have seen and heard: the blind regain their sight, the lame walk, lepers are cleansed, the deaf hear, the dead are raised, the poor have the good news proclaimed to them. And blessed is the one who takes no offense at me.*

—LUKE 7:22–23

How do we keep the faith? Not so much, it seems, by assenting to a set of doctrines but rather by living the way Jesus lived, doing the things Jesus did, and trusting the Father whom Jesus trusted.

Isaiah 45:6–8, 18, 21–25
Psalm 85
Luke 7:18–23

*Enlarge the space for your tent,*
*spread out your tent cloths unsparingly;*
*lengthen your ropes and make firm your stakes.*

—ISAIAH 54:2

When we expand our hearts and minds as the prophet Isaiah urges us to do, we will find that our world includes many people who previously have been excluded.

Jesus' tent knew no limits. It welcomed everyone, especially those whom the "system" excluded.

Isaiah 54:1–10
Psalm 30
Luke 7:24–30

*Friday*

# DECEMBER 17

*In him shall all the tribes of the earth be blessed;
all the nations shall proclaim his happiness.*

—PSALM 72:17

As we approach the Christmas season, let us take just a moment today to listen to the sound of perfect harmony. It needs two voices. The first voice is that of God, who from the very beginning has poured forth blessing on all the peoples of the earth and will never cease to do so. The second voice is that of God's creation, echoing the blessing by living in loving relationship with one another and with God. This may sound like a distant dream, but in fact the music of blessing begins right now and right here, every time we set aside our narrow tribalism and relate to one another with love.

Genesis 49:2, 8–10
Psalm 72
Matthew 1:1–17

*Behold, the days are coming, says the LORD,*
*when I will raise up a righteous shoot to David;*
*As king he shall reign and govern wisely,*
*he shall do what is just and right in the land.*

—JEREMIAH 23:5

That shoot will become the root of everything humanity can become, and that root will bear branches, and those branches will bear fruit: the fruit of honesty and integrity.

Each of us is called to be a branch.

Jeremiah 23:5–8
Psalm 72
Matthew 1:18–25

*The virgin shall conceive, and bear a son, and shall name him Emmanuel.*

—ISAIAH 7:14

*Emmanuel* means "God-with-us": not some distant dream, but a statement of fact that is always true. We could never have grasped this truth until we saw the reality of it, lying in a manger.

Isaiah 7:10–14
Psalm 24
Romans 1:1–7
Matthew 1:18–24

# DECEMBER 20

*Elizabeth, your relative, has also conceived a son in her old age, and this is the sixth month for her who was called barren; for nothing will be impossible for God.*

—LUKE 1:36–37

Susan often thought back over her long life as she sat, lonely and forgotten, in the nursing home, day after tedious day. *What point has there been in all of it?* she wondered. Her days had been fruitless, meaningless. Her life had made no difference.

Then a letter came from a former pupil, thanking Susan for all she had meant to him. Just a sheet of paper—but a spark of life, direct from God, redeeming her barrenness, setting her heart alight with meaning and significance.

Isaiah 7:10–14
Psalm 24
Luke 1:26–38

*When Elizabeth heard Mary's greeting, the infant leaped in her womb,*
*and Elizabeth [was] filled with the Holy Spirit.*

—LUKE 1:41

God's call, however faintly we may perceive it, quivers
through our being with a joy and an insistence that shakes
us into life.

Take time to remember when you have felt the quiver of
God's touch on your life.

Song of Songs 2:8–14 or Zephaniah 3:14–18
Psalm 33
Luke 1:39–45

# DECEMBER 22

*He has cast down the mighty from their thrones*
*and has lifted up the lowly.*
*He has filled the hungry with good things,*
*and the rich he has sent away empty.*

—LUKE 1:52–53

God's justice turns our systems upside down.

God's integrity turns our values inside out.

1 Samuel 1:24–28
1 Samuel 2:1, 4–8
Luke 1:46–56

*[The father] asked for a tablet and wrote, "John is his name," and all were amazed. Immediately his mouth was opened, his tongue freed, and he spoke blessing God.*

—LUKE 1:63–64

When I do what I know in my heart I must do, then my life will speak its own truth.

Malachi 3:1–4, 23–24
Psalm 25
Luke 1:57–66

*You, my child, shall be called prophet of the Most High,*
*for you will go before the Lord to prepare his way.*

—LUKE 1:76

Every day of every life is a call to make choices and
decisions that help to prepare the way of the Lord. Every
choice to do the more loving thing is a paving stone on
that way.

2 Samuel 7:1–5, 8–12, 14, 16
Psalm 89
Luke 1:67–79

# DECEMBER 25

• THE NATIVITY OF THE LORD • CHRISTMAS •

*The people who walked in darkness*
*have seen a great light;*
*Upon those who dwelt in the land of gloom*
*a light has shone.*

—ISAIAH 9:1

Dazzled by the false lights of our own imagined glory, we
stumble and fall because in truth our own light is darkness.
But we find the true light in the darkness of God's mystery
is where the true light is to be found.

| **Vigil** | **Dawn** |
|---|---|
| Isaiah 62:1–5 | Isaiah 62:11–12 |
| Psalm 89 | Psalm 97 |
| Acts 13:16–17, 22–25 | Titus 3:4–7 |
| Matthew 1:1–25 or 1:18–25 | Luke 2:15–20 |
| **Midnight** | **Day** |
| Isaiah 9:1–6 | Isaiah 52:7–10 |
| Psalm 96 | Psalm 98 |
| Titus 2:11–14 | Hebrews 1:1–6 |
| Luke 2:1–14 | John 1:1–18 or 1:1–5, 9–14 |

# DECEMBER 26

• THE HOLY FAMILY OF JESUS, MARY, AND JOSEPH •

*When the magi had departed, behold, the angel of the Lord appeared
to Joseph in a dream and said, "Rise, take the child and his mother, flee
to Egypt, and stay there until I tell you. Herod is going to search for
the child to destroy him." . . . When Herod had died, behold, the angel
of the Lord appeared in a dream to Joseph in Egypt and said, "Rise,
take the child and his mother and go to the land of Israel, for those who
sought the child's life are dead."*

—MATTHEW 2:13, 19–20

Sometimes the slenderest of dreams is all that separates the
path of destruction from the path of life.

Which of our dreams are of God? Which dreams shall
we trust?

Sirach 3:2–7, 12–14
Psalm 128
Colossians 3:12–21 or 3:12–17
Matthew 2:13–15, 19–23

*What was from the beginning,*
*what we have heard,*
*what we have seen with our eyes,*
*what we looked upon*
*and touched with our hands*
*concerns the Word of life.*

—1 JOHN 1:1

The eternal Word is not some abstraction of philosophy or theology. It is something we can see and observe in action, something we can touch with our own hands. It lies all around us, in the vulnerable lives of our brothers and sisters and in the fragile beauty of a living planet. Its echo resounds in our own words. Its power has chosen to reside in our shaky hands.

1 John 1:1–4
Psalm 97
John 20:1a,2–8

# DECEMBER 28

• THE HOLY INNOCENTS, MARTYRS •

*A voice was heard in Ramah,*
*sobbing and loud lamentation:*
*Rachel weeping for her children,*
*and she would not be consoled,*
*since they were no more.*

—MATTHEW 2:18

And still the heart-rending lament of a million Rachels fills the airwaves and the newspapers. Dare we let it pierce our hearts? Or will we collude with the systems of destruction? It seems that we must decide, one way or the other; there is no fence to sit on.

1 John 1:5—2:2
Psalm 124
Matthew 2:13–18

*I do write a new commandment to you,*
*which holds true in him and among you,*
*for the darkness is passing away,*
*and the true light is already shining.*

—1 JOHN 2:8

The light of the nations has also kindled a little candle flame in our own lives. It will guide us through whatever lies ahead. It will never be extinguished. We can follow the commandment to love and to live in peace, because we know that God is fulfilling God's promise in our lives.

1 John 2:3–11
Psalm 96
Luke 2:22–35

*When they had fulfilled all the prescriptions of the law of the Lord, they returned to Galilee, to their own town of Nazareth. The child grew and became strong, filled with wisdom; and the favor of God was upon him.*

—LUKE 2:39–40

We, too, are called to grow toward the fullness of everything God knows we can become. The place where this quiet growth will happen is back in Galilee, in the circumstances and situations of everyday life, in the deep recesses of our own hearts, and in the way we choose to live each moment.

1 John 2:12–17
Psalm 96
Luke 2:36–40

# DECEMBER 31

*Sing to the LORD a new song;*
*sing to the LORD, all you lands.*
*Sing to the LORD; bless his name;*
*announce his salvation, day after day.*

—PSALM 96:1–2

We stand on the threshold of a new year. We look back with thanksgiving on all the events of 2010 that have brought us to this new place. We pause for a while, to say to God whatever we need to say, by way of regret and gratitude. Then we turn to greet a whole new beginning, to embrace 365 new days with trust and courage, while singing a new song, together.

1 John 2:18–21
Psalm 96
John 1:1–18

*And Mary kept all these things, reflecting on them in her heart.*
—LUKE 2:19

Just as a seed grows slowly and steadily in the darkness of the wintering earth, so the seed of wisdom grows in the depths of our pondering hearts if we allow God to plant it there and if we water it with reflection.

Numbers 6:22–27
Psalm 67
Galatians 4:4–7
Luke 2:16–21

# JANUARY 2

• EPIPHANY OF THE LORD •

*And behold, the star that they had seen at its rising preceded them, until
it came and stopped over the place where the child was.*

—MATTHEW 2:9

The beam of God's light is always there to guide us, but
all too often the clouds of our own concerns and anxieties
obscure it and leave us wandering in the shadows.

Isaiah 60:1–6
Psalm 72
Ephesians 3:2–3, 5–6
Matthew 2:1–12

*From that time on, Jesus began to preach and say, "Repent, for the Kingdom of heaven is at hand."*

—MATTHEW 4:16–17

The French word for sunflower is *tournesol*—that which turns toward the sun. A sunflower will always strive to turn its head toward the source of light. We, too, once we have recognized the source that is the light of life, are to become sunflowers, seeking always to gaze in the direction of that light and let it guide our steps. To repent is to practice this turning of heart and mind every day of our lives.

1 John 3:22—4:6
Psalm 2
Matthew 4:12–17, 23–25

# JANUARY 4

*By now it was already late and his disciples approached him and said,*
*"This is a deserted place and it is already very late. Dismiss them*
*so that they can go to the surrounding farms and villages and buy*
*themselves something to eat." He said to them in reply, "Give them some*
*food yourselves."*

—MARK 6:35–37

Sometimes God challenges us to become the answers to
our own prayers. When we ask God to comfort, support,
or nourish those in need, dare we allow ourselves to hear
the response "Give them something to eat yourselves"?
When we hear and respond, that might just be the start of
a miracle.

1 John 4:7–10
Psalm 72
Mark 6:34–44

*There is no fear in love, but perfect love drives out fear because fear has to do with punishment, and so one who fears is not yet perfect in love.*

—1 JOHN 4:18

Fear is the greatest enemy of love. If fear creeps into a human relationship, then love leaves by the back door.

There's a reason "don't be afraid" is one of the most commonly repeated phrases in Scripture. Let us be sure, then, that if anything at all is causing us to be fearful, in expectation of punishment, it is not coming from God.

1 John 4:11–18
Psalm 72
Mark 6:45–52

*If anyone says, "I love God," but hates his brother, he is a liar; for whoever does not love a brother whom he has seen cannot love God whom he has not seen.*

—1 JOHN 4:20

If I spend all night on my knees in prayer but the next morning I lash out at my children or kick my cat, I am very far from loving God. But if I go out of my way to help a neighbor, to sit with my children as they do their homework, to write a note of encouragement to someone who is hurting, then I am loving God even though I may not have had a spare moment all day for formal prayer.

1 John 4:19—5:4
Psalm 72
Luke 4:14–22

*The report about [Jesus] spread all the more, and great crowds assembled to listen to him and to be cured of their ailments, but he would withdraw to deserted places to pray.*

—LUKE 5:15–16

To live out our calling to be the people God created us to be, we need to be a bit like the wick in an oil lamp. One end of the wick needs to be immersed in the oil; only then can flame come to the end that is extended into the room beyond. If Jesus needed to keep taking time to be alone in prayer, immersing himself in the oil of God's presence to supply the fuel of his ministry, how much more do we need to do the same?

1 John 5:5–13
Psalm 147
Luke 5:12–16

# JANUARY 8

*No one can receive anything except what has been given from heaven.*
—JOHN 3:27

Everything we own on this earth has been given us by God. All is pure gift. Even the things we have bought with money we have earned are ours only because we have used our gifts to earn them. The only thing we can ever add to the abundance of all we have been given is love—the love that urges us to spend our gifts for the greater good of all creation.

1 John 5:14–21
Psalm 149
John 3:22–30

*Jesus came from Galilee to John at the Jordan to be baptized by him.*
*John tried to prevent him, saying, "I need to be baptized by you, and*
*yet you are coming to me?"*

—MATTHEW 3:13–14

Jesus, the one who made the stars, turns all our
expectations on their heads, coming to us, to invite us to
come to him.

Isaiah 42:1–4, 6–7
Psalm 29
Acts 10:34–38
Matthew 3:13–17

# JANUARY 10

*Brothers and sisters: In times past, God spoke in partial and various ways to our ancestors through the prophets; in these last days, he spoke to us through the Son, whom he made heir of all things and through whom he created the universe.*

—HEBREWS 1:1–2

And still today we know that God speaks—through Scriptures and the life of Christ's body, the church. The Holy speaks wherever we see people bringing hope to those who have nothing, release to those in the bondage of fear, insight to those who are blinded, and new possibilities of life to those whose will to live has been crushed.

Hebrews 1:1–6
Psalm 97
Mark 1:14–20

# JANUARY 11

*Jesus came to Capernaum with his followers, and on the sabbath he entered the synagogue and taught. The people were astonished at his teaching, for he taught them as one having authority and not as the scribes.*

—MARK 1:21–22

How do we know today when we are hearing teaching that carries true authority? If teaching truly comes from God, it will resonate within us, thrill us to the core, and set our hearts on fire. Such teaching will impel us to take what we have received and give it to a needy world, thus allowing it to become a reality in our own time and place.

Hebrews 2:5–12
Psalm 8
Mark 1:21–28

*Simon and those who were with him pursued him and on finding him said, "Everyone is looking for you." He told them, "Let us go on to the nearby villages that I may preach there also. For this purpose have I come."*

—MARK 1:36–38

The farmer does not plant all the seed in one corner of the field but sows it everywhere, so that the crop might grow and flourish freely and bring sustenance to all, wherever they are.

Hebrews 2:14–18
Psalm 105
Mark 1:29–39

*Oh, that today you would hear his voice:*
*"Harden not your hearts."*
—PSALM 95:7–8

How strange that so often we become sensitive to God's
voice and to the cries of one another only when our hearts
have been softened by sorrow. May we have the grace
to embrace the sorrows that life brings us and let them
soften—not harden—our hearts.

Hebrews 3:7–14
Psalm 95
Mark 1:40–45

# JANUARY 14

*What we have heard and know,*
*and what our fathers declared to us,*
*we will declare to the generation to come.*

—PSALM 78:3–4

If we were to stop educating our children in the ways of life, all human progress would end in one generation.

If we fail to pass on the sacred story of how God has traveled with us, we will be leaving our children in a cul-de-sac of meaninglessness.

Hebrews 4:1–5, 11
Psalm 78
Mark 2:1–12

---

# JANUARY 15

*The word of God is living and effective, sharper than any two-edged sword, penetrating even between soul and spirit, joints and marrow, and able to discern reflections and thoughts of the heart.*

—HEBREWS 4:12

A friend's comment, a critic's warning, a child's unwitting observation—all are ways in which God's living blade pierces my heart. It pierces not to harm but to heal me, not to sever but to reconnect my heart to God's.

Hebrews 4:12–16
Psalm 19
Mark 2:13–17

# JANUARY 16

*Sacrifice and offering you wished not,*
*but ears open to obedience you gave me.*
*Holocausts or sin-offerings you sought not;*
*then said I, "Behold I come."*
—PSALM 40:7

All my doings will never bring me closer to you Lord.
What you are asking is my being.

Isaiah 49:3, 5–6
Psalm 40
1 Corinthians 1:1–3
John 1:29–34

*"No one pours new wine into old wineskins. Otherwise, the wine will burst the skins, and both the wine and the skins are ruined. Rather, new wine is poured into fresh wineskins."*

—MARK 2:22

Fresh skins—that is, new ways of speaking and living the good news—may be challenging to us. Do we dare risk them?

Or, do we dare not take the risk?

Hebrews 5:1–10
Psalm 110
Mark 2:18–22

*"The sabbath was made for man, not man for the sabbath. That is why the Son of Man is lord even of the sabbath."*

—MARK 2:27

The riverbank guides and restrains the course of the river, but the river itself is what brings life. In the same way, we need rules for guidance, but only if they serve life.

Hebrews 6:10–20
Psalm 111
Mark 2:23–28

# JANUARY 19

*Looking around at them with anger and grieved at their hardness of heart, Jesus said to the man, "Stretch out your hand." He stretched it out and his hand was restored.*

—MARK 3:5

The wholeness that God offers sometimes requires that we boldly reach out to receive it. Then we must stretch out to share it with one another.

Hebrews 7:1–3, 15–17
Psalm 110
Mark 3:1–6

*[Jesus] told his disciples to have a boat ready for him because of the crowd, so that they would not crush him.*

—MARK 3:9

Jesus took refuge on a boat because the pressures of other people threatened to crush him. When do the pressures of others threaten to crush you? And where do you find refuge when that happens? If Jesus needed refuge, then certainly we do.

Hebrews 7:25—8:6
Psalm 40
Mark 3:7–12

# JANUARY 21

• ST. AGNES, VIRGIN AND MARTYR •

*I will put my laws in their minds
and I will write them upon their hearts.
I will be their God,
and they shall be my people.*
—HEBREWS 8:10

Fear of punishment might compel us to keep the external laws. But only love will lead us to honor the law that God has engraved personally on our hearts. Coercion may lead to obedience, but attraction will take us beyond obedience to joyful service.

Hebrews 8:6–13
Psalm 85
Mark 3:13–19

*Jesus came with his disciples into the house. Again the crowd gathered, making it impossible for them even to eat. When his relatives heard of this they set out to seize him, for they said, "He is out of his mind."*

—MARK 3:20–21

Pioneers and prophets are always out of step. Even their families think so—especially their families!

Hebrews 9:2–3, 11–14
Psalm 47
Mark 3:20–21

# JANUARY 23

*As he was walking by the Sea of Galilee, [Jesus] saw two brothers, Simon who is called Peter, and his brother Andrew, casting a net into the sea; they were fishermen. He said to them, "Come after me, and I will make you fishers of men."*

—MATTHEW 4:18–19

Jesus often calls us to do for God what we are already gifted and skilled to do—but differently. It usually isn't a call to do something wildly different but a call to change our focus from ourselves to others and to God.

Isaiah 8:23—9:3
Psalm 27
1 Corinthians 1:10–13, 17
Matthew 4:12–23 or 4:12–17

*If a kingdom is divided against itself, that kingdom cannot stand. And if a house is divided against itself, that house will not be able to stand.*

—MARK 3:24–25

As long as I focus on what is best for me, I potentially put myself into conflict with every other person. When *I* gives way to *us*, the divisions can be transcended and a deeper unity of heart can emerge.

Hebrews 9:15, 24–28
Psalm 98
Mark 3:22–30

*On that journey as I drew near to Damascus, about noon a great light from the sky suddenly shone around me. I fell to the ground and heard a voice saying to me, "Saul, Saul, why are you persecuting me?" I replied, "Who are you, sir?" And he said to me, "I am Jesus the Nazorean whom you are persecuting." My companions saw the light but did not hear the voice of the one who spoke to me.*

—ACTS 22:6–9

When the light overwhelms Saul, he is a notorious persecutor of the Christians. But the light that robs him of his sight also opens his heart. He hears the stupendous truth about the reality of Jesus, who lives on and continues to be persecuted in our own times, sometimes with our collusion. In that new knowledge, Saul directs his energy to working with, rather than against, God.

Acts 22:3–16 or 9:1–22
Psalm 117
Mark 16:15–18

*I remind you to stir into flame the gift of God that you have through the imposition of my hands. For God did not give us a spirit of cowardice but rather of power and love and self-control.*

—2 TIMOTHY 1:6–7

There is something in each of us—in the core of our being—that springs from the timeless mystery deeper than consciousness, higher than knowledge, and more alive than our physical presence. In that mystery alone will we discover who we truly are.

2 Timothy 1:1–8 or Titus 1:1–5
Psalm 96
Mark 4:1–20

# JANUARY 27

*Is a lamp brought in to be placed under a bushel basket or under a bed,
and not to be placed on a lampstand? For there is nothing hidden except
to be made visible; nothing is secret except to come to light.*

—MARK 4:21–22

We might not stow the lamp away under the bed, but
often we push our gifts away into a dark, unacknowledged
corner because of false modesty. How different this world
might be if we could embrace our gifts for what they are—
gifts, not achievements—and then use them freely and
joyfully wherever they are needed.

Hebrews 10:19–25
Psalm 24
Mark 4:21–25

*This is how it is with the Kingdom of God; it is as if a man were to scatter seed on the land and would sleep and rise night and day and the seed would sprout and grow, he knows not how.*

—MARK 4:26–27

It's winter. The land is ice bound, and my garden is frozen hard. I gaze out at the lifeless scene beyond my window, and I know that deep in the soil the daffodils are preparing for rebirth.

Perhaps God looks upon our frozen hearts in the same way and knows already what we can only hope for.

Hebrews 10:32–39
Psalm 37
Mark 4:26–34

*All these died in faith. They did not receive what had been promised but saw it and greeted it from afar and acknowledged themselves to be strangers and aliens on earth.*

—HEBREWS 11:13

The journey of faith is always going to be moving on toward a distant horizon. If we think we have arrived, we may well have lost our way.

Hebrews 11:1–2, 8–19
Luke 1:69–75
Mark 4:35–41

# JANUARY 30

*God chose the foolish of the world to shame the wise, and God chose the weak of the world to shame the strong, and God chose the lowly and despised of the world, those who count for nothing, to reduce to nothing those who are something.*

—1 CORINTHIANS 1:27–28

Spiritual growth usually happens not on the peaks of achievement but in the depths of failure and the valley of helplessness.

Spiritual giants are usually those who have come to know, and learned to trust, the God of the depths. Such are the ones whom God can use.

Zephaniah 2:3; 3:12–13
Psalm 146
1 Corinthians 1:26–31
Matthew 5:1–12

# JANUARY 31

*Once I said in my anguish,*
*"I am cut off from your sight";*
*Yet you heard the sound of my pleading*
*when I cried out to you.*

—PSALM 31:23

A panic erupts. The car has broken down in the middle of nowhere, and there is no cell phone signal. We are out of range of emergency assistance. Ten years ago there were no cell phones. A hundred years ago there were no cars.

Yet for thousands of years men and women have known God's response to their pleading—the response of One who is never out of range and who needs no invention of ours to be eternally present to our cries.

Hebrews 11:32–40
Psalm 31
Mark 5:1–20

# FEBRUARY 1

*He took along the child's father and mother and those who were with him and entered the room where the child was. He took the child by the hand and said to her, "Talitha koum!" which means, "Little girl, I say to you, arise!" The girl, a child of twelve, arose immediately and walked around.*

—MARK 5:40–42

Dare I allow Jesus to take the hand of the frightened little girl who still cowers in my heart?

Will she hear his invitation and risk responding to the One who can lead her to the woman God is dreaming her to be?

Hebrews 12:1–4
Psalm 22
Mark 5:21–43

*Now, Master, you may let your servant go
in peace, according to your word,
for my eyes have seen your salvation,
which you prepared in sight of all the peoples,
a light for revelation to the Gentiles,
and glory for your people Israel.*

—LUKE 2:29–32

According to one European tradition, Christmas
decorations—especially the Christmas manger—are
dismantled on the feast of the Presentation of the Lord and
stowed away until next year. When I honor this custom,
it feels like an echo of Simeon's words in the temple.
Now God can let us go—into the world of the new year,
knowing that God is truly incarnate in all our pathways.

Malachi 3:1–4
Psalm 24
Hebrews 2:14–18
Luke 2:22–40 or 2:22–32

*[Jesus] instructed them to take nothing for the journey but a walking stick—no food, no sack, no money in their belts.*

*—MARK 6:8*

God obviously likes emptiness in which to work: empty wombs, empty stables, empty tombs, and empty hearts. So why do I think I need so much baggage for the journey? Why do I think I need to fill up my empty spaces instead of leaving myself open and free to receive God's flow of grace?

Hebrews 12:18–19, 21–24
Psalm 48
Mark 6:7–13

*Let brotherly love continue. Do not neglect hospitality, for through it some have unknowingly entertained angels.*

—HEBREWS 13:1–2

Perhaps one of the greatest gifts the angels give us is their ability to keep discovering new disguises in which to appear at our door.

Hebrews 13:1–8
Psalm 27
Mark 6:14–29

*The Apostles gathered together with Jesus and reported all they had done and taught. He said to them, "Come away by yourselves to a deserted place and rest a while."*

—MARK 6:30–31

Over all our restless doing, God spreads the blanket of simply being and bids us to rest a while!

Hebrews 13:15–17, 20–21
Psalm 23
Mark 6:30–34

# FEBRUARY 6

• ST. PAUL MIKI AND COMPANIONS, MARTYRS •

*You are the salt of the earth. But if salt loses its taste, with what can it be seasoned? It is no longer good for anything but to be thrown out and trampled underfoot.*

—MATTHEW 5:13

Living in "the now" means pouring out our gifts for one another today, because tomorrow they may have lost their effectiveness, and next week they may be gone.

Isaiah 58:7–10
Psalm 112
1 Corinthians 2:1–5
Matthew 5:13–16

# FEBRUARY 7

*Whatever villages or towns or countryside he entered, they laid the
sick in the marketplaces and begged him that they might touch only the
tassel on his cloak; and as many as touched it were healed.*

—MARK 6:56

I reach out, feebly, in my prayer, to touch the fringe of
your cloak, and only then do I realize that it is actually
*you*, who are constantly reaching out to touch *me* with your
healing love.

Genesis 1:1–19
Psalm 104
Mark 6:53–56

# FEBRUARY 8

• ST. JEROME EMILIANI, PRIEST • ST. JOSEPHINE BAKHITA, VIRGIN •

*This people honors me with their lips,*
*but their hearts are far from me;*
*In vain do they worship me,*
*teaching as doctrines human precepts.*

—MARK 7:6–7

Jesus isn't talking about us, is he? Surely not us! Dear God,
please lead us beyond the entanglements we have tied
around our own feet and the many words with which we
cover up your silence.

Genesis 1:20—2:4
Psalm 8
Mark 7:1–13

*Do you not realize that everything that goes into a person from outside cannot defile, since it enters not the heart but the stomach and passes out into the latrine? . . . But what comes out of the man, that is what defiles him.*

—MARK 7:18–20

The real weapons of mass destruction are not the threats, real or imagined, from "enemy states" but the countless spiteful comments, cruel jibes, and sarcastic remarks that we aim at one another every day.

Genesis 2:4–9, 15–17
Psalm 104
Mark 7:14–23

# FEBRUARY 10

• ST. SCHOLASTICA, VIRGIN •

*[Jesus] said to [the Syrophoenician woman], "Let the children be fed first. For it is not right to take the food of the children and throw it to the dogs." She replied and said to him, "Lord, even the dogs under the table eat the children's scraps."*

—MARK 7:27–28

A feisty woman challenges the status quo, and Jesus allows her to stretch the boundaries to include us all. Where are the boundaries now? And are they fixed or flexible? These are big questions—for every new generation.

Genesis 2:18–25
Psalm 128
Mark 7:24–30

*[Jesus] took him off by himself away from the crowd. He put his finger into the man's ears and, spitting, touched his tongue; then he looked up to heaven and groaned, and said to him, "Ephphatha!"*
*(that is, "Be opened!")*

—MARK 7:33–34

Not through intellectual striving but only in the deepest intimacy of God's personal touch upon us will our eyes and ears be opened to see God's presence, to hear God's word, and to respond to God's love in our lives.

Genesis 3:1–8
Psalm 32
Mark 7:31–37

*Teach us to number our days aright,*
*that we may gain wisdom of heart.*
—PSALM 90:12

When crisis takes hold of us, and life itself is under
threat, our whole focus narrows and sharpens to just a
single point. At that point the beam of God's wisdom can
penetrate our hearts like a laser beam and open up a whole
new dimension of our humanity.

Genesis 3:9–24
Psalm 90
Mark 8:1–10

*You have heard that it was said to your ancestors, "You shall not kill;
and whoever kills will be liable to judgment." But I say to you, whoever
is angry with his brother will be liable to judgment.*

—MATTHEW 5:21–22

Every act of violence begins with a small destructive
movement in the heart. We can do very little to stem the
tide of violence in a troubled world, but we can do a great
deal to address the small destructive movements that stir in
our own troubled hearts.

Sirach 15:15–20
Psalm 119
1 Corinthians 2:6–10
Matthew 5:17–37 or 5:20–22, 27–28, 33–34, 37

*Then the LORD asked Cain, "Where is your brother Abel?" He answered, "I do not know. Am I my brother's keeper?" The LORD then said: "What have you done! Listen: your brother's blood cries out to me from the soil!"*

—GENESIS 4:9–10

The television news cries out to us in the sheltered comfort of our homes: What have you done? Can't you hear your brother's blood crying out to you from the world's killing-fields?

"It wasn't me, Lord. It wasn't us. These are other people, other places, other problems." We switch off the television, but the voice of reproach continues, whether or not we listen and agree. We are our brother's keeper.

Genesis 4:1–15, 25
Psalm 50
Mark 8:11–13

---

*Do you not yet understand or comprehend? Are your hearts hardened?*
*Do you have eyes and not see, ears and not hear? And do you not*
*remember . . . ?*

—MARK 8:17–18

Perhaps we're not blind, but certainly we're shortsighted,
because our eyes are focused on our own immediate wants
and wishes.

Perhaps we're not deaf, but certainly we suffer from
selective hearing, listening to what gives us comfort and
filtering out what challenges us.

Genesis 6:5–8; 7:1–5, 10
Psalm 29
Mark 8:14–21

*As long as the earth lasts,*
*seedtime and harvest,*
*cold and heat,*
*Summer and winter,*
*and day and night*
*shall not cease.*

—GENESIS 8:22

In times of change or disaster, what once seemed so fixed and certain now raises many questions. Yet we can trust that the deep wisdom that holds all things in existence also holds us, through everything that life can throw at us. This wisdom enfolds us in a love that will not let us go, even though the earth itself may crumble.

Genesis 8:6–13, 20–22
Psalm 116
Mark 8:22–26

# FEBRUARY 17

*I set my bow in the clouds to serve as a sign of the covenant between me and the earth.*

—GENESIS 9:13

How often has a rainbow appeared in a stormy sky just when I needed to hear its eternal promise? Yet that promise needs both sunshine and rain, my sorrow and my joy, to reveal itself.

Genesis 9:1–13
Psalm 102
Mark 8:27–33

*What profit is there for one to gain the whole world and forfeit his life?*
*What could one give in exchange for his life?*

—MARK 8:36–37

Very few people at the end of life wish they had spent more time at work, banked more dollars, or had a bigger house. But many regret that they didn't spend more time living, loving, enjoying God's earth, and cherishing God's people.

Genesis 11:1–9
Psalm 33
Mark 8:34—9:1

*Faith is the realization of what is hoped for and evidence of things not seen.*

—HEBREWS 11:1

Science explores all that can be observed, tested, and measured. Faith explores the things we know are real but can't be seen, such as love and trust, hope and goodness.

Science and faith are not opponents but indispensable partners in our quest to discover who we truly are and to live our humanity to the fullest.

Hebrews 11:1–7
Psalm 145
Mark 9:2–13

# FEBRUARY 20

*You have heard that it was said, "You shall love your neighbor and hate your enemy." But I say to you, love your enemies, and pray for those who persecute you.*

—MATTHEW 5:43–44

Psychiatrist and author M. Scott Peck and others have said that love is not an emotion; it is a decision. We may not feel love for those who do us harm, but we always have the freedom to choose to behave toward them in the most loving way we can.

Leviticus 19:1–2, 17–18
Psalm 103
1 Corinthians 3:16–23
Matthew 5:38–48

*Before all things else wisdom was created;*
*and prudent understanding, from eternity.*
*To whom has wisdom's root been revealed?*
*Who knows her subtleties?*

—SIRACH 1:4–5

In the scuttling of the ants and the wheeling of the stars, in the epic journeys of migrating birds and the unfolding wonders of an evolving universe, in the grip of a baby's finger and the lines in an old man's face—in all these things we see the fingerprints of a wisdom whose root we can never uncover.

Sirach 1:1–10
Psalm 93
Mark 9:14–29

# FEBRUARY 22

• CHAIR OF ST. PETER, APOSTLE •

*The LORD is my shepherd; I shall not want.*

—PSALM 23:1

At a parish celebration, a renowned actor was invited and asked to recite this psalm. He did so beautifully, and the people were impressed, but then he turned to the humble pastor and asked him to recite it also. The pastor was embarrassed, but he did his best in his modest manner, and the people were spellbound.

Then the actor said to the people, "You see, my friends. I know the psalm, but your pastor here—he knows the shepherd."

1 Peter 5:1–4
Psalm 23
Matthew 16:13–19

# FEBRUARY 23

• ST. POLYCARP, BISHOP AND MARTYR •

*Wisdom instructs her children and admonishes those who seek her.*
—SIRACH 4:11

External controls and sanctions may keep us in line and compliant with authority.

But only a deep and inward relationship with God will bring us to the maturity of our full humanity.

Sirach 4:11–19
Psalm 119
Mark 9:38–40

# FEBRUARY 24

*Rely not on your wealth;*
*say not: "I have the power."*
*Rely not on your strength*
*in following the desires of your heart.*
—SIRACH 5:1–2

At the click of a mouse on Wall Street, our financial
security can disappear in minutes.

Will our hearts go with it? Our compassion, our resilience,
our faith?

Sirach 5:1–8
Psalm 1
Mark 9:41–50

# FEBRUARY 25

*A kind mouth multiplies friends and appeases enemies,*
*and gracious lips prompt friendly greetings.*
—SIRACH 6:5

Through coercive and manipulative speech, we can get
people to go along with us, to a point. But when we
express kindness and graciousness, the hearts of others will
open to us like flower petals to the sun.

Sirach 6:5–17
Psalm 119
Mark 10:1–12

⇒ 90 ⇐

# FEBRUARY 26

*Amen, I say to you, whoever does not accept the Kingdom of God like a child will not enter it.*

—MARK 10:15

When I was a child, I knew beyond any question that God lived in the woods at the end of our garden, and I used to go there often and talk to him. Then my elders came along and taught me what I was to believe about this God, and it was then that things started to unravel into questions and doubts. It took me years to reconnect to the God who had always been there, waiting for me to return to simplicity of a heart-knowledge that would always be more powerful, more real, than all the questions.

Sirach 17:1–15
Psalm 103
Mark 10:13–16

# FEBRUARY 27

*Do not worry about tomorrow; tomorrow will take care of itself.*
*Sufficient for a day is its own evil.*
—MATTHEW 6:34

How often do I ask myself, "Where has the day gone?"
The truth is that half of it was spent regretting yesterday,
and half of it leaked away in anxieties about tomorrow.
Perhaps my evening prayer should reflect on the question,
Did I actually live today?

Isaiah 49:14–15
Psalm 62
1 Corinthians 4:1–5
Matthew 6:24–34

*Jesus again said to them . . . "Children, how hard it is to enter the Kingdom of God! It is easier for a camel to pass through the eye of a needle than for one who is rich to enter the Kingdom of God."*

—MARK 10:24–25

How often I hear the cabin crew in an aircraft warn passengers: "In the event of an emergency, don't inflate your life jacket before leaving the plane."

It sounds so obvious: of course an inflated life jacket would prevent you from getting out of the aircraft. And just as obviously, an inflated ego, with all its baggage, will prevent us from entering the kingdom of God.

Sirach 17:20–24
Psalm 32
Mark 10:17–27

# MARCH 1

*Many that are first will be last, and the last will be first.*

—MARK 10:31

My achievements may fill up my résumé, but they may also clog up my mind and heart and impede the flow of the Holy Spirit through my life's situations. What gives us prestige in the world is usually not what truly makes our life meaningful in God's view.

Sirach 35:1–12
Psalm 50
Mark 10:28–31

*Whoever wishes to be great among you will be your servant; whoever wishes to be first among you will be the slave of all.*

—MARK 10:43–44

Those who are the least full of themselves will be the ones who have the most room for others, and for God.

Sirach 36:1, 4–5, 10–17
Psalm 79
Mark 10:32–45

*Jesus said [to the blind Bartimaeus], "What do you want me to do for you?" The blind man replied to him, "Master, I want to see."*

—MARK 10:51

The first step to healing is the realization of how much I need it. As long as I think I can see, God cannot heal my blindness.

Sirach 42:15–25
Psalm 33
Mark 10:46–52

*Have faith in God. Amen, I say to you, whoever says to this mountain,*
*"Be lifted up and thrown into the sea," and does not doubt in his heart*
*but believes that what he says will happen, it shall be done for him.*

—MARK 11:22–23

Every cell in my body entrusts itself to the greater wisdom
of the whole. That is, my body's cells work according to a
design that is greater than any one cell. In the same way,
every star in the universe trusts the wisdom of the cosmos
that holds it in existence.

Why would I think I am an exception to the cosmic rule?
Why do I shrink back from trusting the Wisdom that
overarches the world and yet holds me so gently?

Sirach 44:1, 9–13
Psalm 149
Mark 11:11–26

*As [Jesus] was walking in the temple area, the chief priests, the scribes, and the elders approached him and said to him, "By what authority are you doing these things? Or who gave you this authority to do them?"*

—MARK 11:27–28

Those who questioned Jesus had in mind the authority of human councils and familiar religious systems. Jesus knew that the only authority that counts is that which comes from the author of our being.

Sirach 51:12–20
Psalm 19
Mark 11:27–33

*Everyone who listens to these words of mine but does not act on them
will be like a fool who built his house on sand.*

—MATTHEW 7:26

We can listen and listen to wisdom and truth. We can
agree and argue on the side of wisdom and truth. But our
actions—not our words—make the truth real. Jesus knew
that it's easier to build sandcastles out of words than to
build a real life out of daily labors and actions.

Deuteronomy 11:18, 26–28, 32
Psalm 31
Romans 3:21–25, 28
Matthew 7:21–27

*Monday*

# MARCH 7

*The stone that the builders rejected*
*has become the cornerstone;*
*by the Lord has this been done,*
*and it is wonderful in our eyes.*
—MARK 12:10–11

Jasmine came into the world with significant birth defects.
Her parents and the medics could have let her die. Instead,
they cherished her, and she became the light of life around
which the whole family found its spiritual center.

Tobit 1:3; 2:1–8
Psalm 112
Mark 12:1–12

*Jesus said to them, "Repay to Caesar what belongs to Caesar and to God what belongs to God."*

—MARK 12:17

What Caesar takes is just the outer layers of our life.
They profit him little.

What God asks is the deepest core of who we are, and in
giving this to God, we receive it back a hundredfold.

Tobit 2:9–14
Psalm 112
Mark 12:13–17

*We are ambassadors for Christ, as if God were appealing through us.*
*We implore you on behalf of Christ, be reconciled to God.*

—2 CORINTHIANS 5:20

Christ's embassy would be a place where the discouraged, disaffected, and disempowered could find an unconditional welcome.

Is my heart such a place?

Is my church such a place?

Joel 2:12–18
Psalm 51
2 Corinthians 5:20—6:2
Matthew 6:1–6, 16–18

*I have set before you life and death, the blessing and the curse. Choose life, then, that you and your descendants may live, by loving the LORD, your God, heeding his voice, and holding fast to him.*

—DEUTERONOMY 30:19–20

Choosing life is a moment-by-moment affair: a smile or a rebuff; a word of encouragement or a sarcastic rejoinder; a few minutes of silence in the midst of a busy day; a decision to give instead of take, to understand instead of criticize.

Every personal choice for life makes all of us more fully alive.

Deuteronomy 30:15–20
Psalm 1
Luke 9:22–25

*This . . . is the fasting that I wish: . . .*
*Setting free the oppressed,*
*breaking every yoke;*
*Sharing your bread with the hungry,*
*sheltering the oppressed and the homeless;*
*Clothing the naked when you see them,*
*and not turning your back on your own.*

—ISAIAH 58:6–7

Mike spoke out about the unfair treatment of his colleague.
Jayne took a pot of soup to her elderly neighbor.
Susy knitted socks for refugees.
Brian made sure the scattered family stayed in touch.
They never guessed that they were doing God's work.

Isaiah 58:1–9
Psalm 51
Matthew 9:14–15

*Jesus said . . . "Those who are healthy do not need a physician, but the sick do. I have not come to call the righteous to repentance but sinners."*
—LUKE 5:31–32

God loves a mess: a messy stable, a mixed-up world, a struggling life. Where there is a mess there is also the possibility of an open gateway to grace.

Isaiah 58:9–14
Psalm 86
Luke 5:27–32

# MARCH 13

• FIRST SUNDAY OF LENT •

*One does not live by bread alone,*
*but by every word that comes forth from the mouth of God.*

—MATTHEW 4:4

Jake spent his whole life working to build up savings and possessions. He died in lonely isolation, and only then did he realize how empty his "full-ness" had been.

Genesis 2:7–9, 3:1–7
Psalm 51
Romans 5:12–19 or 5:12, 17–19
Matthew 4:1–11

*Let the words of my mouth and the thought of my heart*
*find favor before you,*
*O LORD, my rock and my redeemer.*

—PSALM 19:15

I will be in harmony with God and with all creation only if what I say and how I live are in harmony with what I know to be true and with whom God has created me to be.

Leviticus 19:1–2, 11–18
Psalm 19
Matthew 25:31–46

# MARCH 15

*The LORD is close to the brokenhearted;*
*and those who are crushed in spirit he saves.*
—PSALM 34:19

It is the broken bread that nourishes the family, and the crushed grape that produces the finest wine.

May we trust God to be with us, in our breaking, our crushing, and our transforming.

Isaiah 55:10–11
Psalm 34
Matthew 6:7–15

# MARCH 16

*A clean heart create for me, O God,*
*and a steadfast spirit renew within me.*
*Cast me not out from your presence,*
*and your Holy Spirit take not from me.*
—PSALM 51:12–13

The hikers were in a hurry. They tried to take their bearings as they walked. They lost their way. If they had taken the time to stand still and read the compass steadily, they would have found their way home.

God never casts us away from God's presence. But there are many times when we walk away from it in our eagerness to do what we want.

Jonah 3:1–10
Psalm 51
Luke 11:29–32

*Do to others whatever you would have them do to you. This is the law and the prophets.*

—MATTHEW 7:12

In every culture and in every faith tradition, the Golden
Rule is the same.
So simple, yet so hard.
So vital to remember, and so easy to neglect.
So sublime in theory. So very difficult in practice.
Impossible. Inescapable.

Esther C:12, 14–16, 23–25
Psalm 138
Matthew 7:7–12

*Out of the depths I cry to you, O LORD;*
*Lord, hear my voice!*
*Let your ears be attentive*
*to my voice in supplication.*
—PSALM 130:1–2

When words fail, when life flounders, and when all hope has fled, then a deep and voiceless cry wells up in the aching center of our soul—and makes its way straight to God's heart.

Ezekiel 18:21–28
Psalm 130
Matthew 5:20–26

*The angel of the Lord appeared to [Joseph] in a dream and said, "Joseph, son of David, do not be afraid to take Mary your wife into your home. For it is through the Holy Spirit that this child has been conceived in her."* . . . *When Joseph awoke, he did as the angel of the Lord had commanded him.*

—MATTHEW 1:20, 24

Joseph is a man who trusts his deepest dream and follows it. God's own dream is given the freedom to come to birth among us whenever we try to be like Joseph; clearing the space for God's will to be done; and doing everything in our power to assist it, even though we may not understand it.

2 Samuel 7:4–5, 12–14, 16
Psalm 89
Romans 4:13, 16–18, 22
Matthew 1:16, 18–21, 24, or Luke 2:41–51

*Our soul waits for the LORD.*

—PSALM 33:20

Waiting can be full of tension or full of joyful anticipation. It depends on who we think we are waiting for.

Are we waiting for one who comes to judge and condemn us or one who comes to liberate and fulfill us?

The one who comes promises that he is coming to give us life in all its fullness. May our waiting reflect the joy that is in that promise.

Genesis 12:1–4
Psalm 33
2 Timothy 1:8–10
Matthew 17:1–9

*Give and gifts will be given to you; a good measure, packed together, shaken down, and overflowing, will be poured into your lap. For the measure with which you measure will in return be measured out to you.*

—LUKE 6:38

The sunflower dropped its beautiful head and gave up all the seeds of itself to the waiting earth.

The next spring there were hundreds of sunflowers on that patch of earth.

Can we, too, give ourselves freely today and trust in the fruits for a tomorrow we may never see?

Daniel 9:4–10
Psalm 79
Luke 6:36–38

*Cease doing evil; learn to do good.*
*Make justice your aim: redress the wronged,*
*hear the orphan's plea, defend the widow.*

—ISAIAH 1:16–17

The law can persuade us to avoid doing what is wrong, but only love can teach us how to do what is good.

The rule of law frees us to engage in the labors of love.

Isaiah 1:10, 16–20
Psalm 50
Matthew 23:1–12

*You know that the rulers of the Gentiles lord it over them, and the great ones make their authority over them felt. But it shall not be so among you.*

—MATTHEW 20:25–26

And if we do see this happening among us—people "leading" by imposing their authority—we will know for sure that this is not of God or of God's kingdom. May we have the courage not to collude with it.

Jeremiah 18:18–20
Psalm 31
Matthew 20:17–28

# MARCH 24

Blessed is the man who trusts in the LORD,
whose hope is the LORD.
He is like a tree planted beside the waters
that stretches out its roots to the stream:
It fears not the heat when it comes,
its leaves stay green;
In the year of drought it shows no distress,
but still bears fruit.

—JEREMIAH 17:7–8

Marie took time each day to go to the deeper center, where she knew God communed with her and where her life was rooted. Whatever happened then, in the outside world, had no power to harm her or rock her inner calm.

Jeremiah 17:5–10
Psalm 1
Luke 16:19–31

*Behold, I come to do your will.*

—HEBREWS 10:9

There is something absolutely unconditional about these words. No ifs or buts or maybes. A simple, unambiguous "yes!" This yes of Jesus is a reflection of Mary's yes when she gave over her life to the will of the One in whom she lived and moved and had her being.

This is all God asks, but it costs everything.

Isaiah 7:10–14; 8:10
Psalm 40
Hebrews 10:4–10
Luke 1:26–38

*Your brother was dead and has come to life again; he was lost and has been found.*

—LUKE 15:32

Sometimes a relationship that seemed long dead can come back to vibrant life if we dare to come home to ourselves and to the other person, in humility, honesty, and goodwill.

Micah 7:14–15, 18–20
Psalm 103
Luke 15:1–3, 11–32

*Whoever drinks the water I shall give will never thirst; the water I shall give will become in him a spring of water welling up to eternal life.*

—JOHN 4:14

We come to you, God, begging for a cupful of grace.

You lead us to your ever-flowing fountain, which springs up out of our true selves as you have created us. In that holy, interior place, if we dare recognize it and drink from it, a fountain exists now and forever.

Exodus 17:3–7
Psalm 95
Romans 5:1–2, 5–8
John 4:5–42 or 4:5–15, 19–26, 39a, 40–42

*Athirst is my soul for God, the living God.*
*When shall I go and behold the face of God?*

—PSALM 42:3

We seem to wait forever outside the door that we believe leads to the presence of God. It can take a lifetime to discover that the handle is on our side of that door. Our hearts are always free to open it and see the face of God smiling blessing upon us.

2 Kings 5:1–15
Psalm 42 and 43
Luke 4:24–30

# MARCH 29

Peter approached Jesus and asked him, "Lord, if my brother sins against me, how often must I forgive him? As many as seven times?" Jesus answered, "I say to you, not seven times but seventy-seven times."

—MATTHEW 18:21–22

To forgive the one who has hurt me is like peeling an onion. I strip off the outer layer and think I have done it. Then I find there is layer upon layer of pain and resentment underneath. Each layer may make me cry again, but it will bring me closer to where I need to be. At that point I may also meet the hearts of those who are trying to forgive me.

Daniel 3:25, 34–43
Psalm 25
Matthew 18:21–35

*Take care and be earnestly on your guard not to forget the things which
your own eyes have seen, nor let them slip from your memory as long
as you live.*

—DEUTERONOMY 4:9

Wisdom is the fruit of experience—but only experience
that we have reflected on and learned from. Let us
therefore be mindful of every moment, ready to harvest its
treasure, heed its warning, and respond to its call to choose
the more loving and life-giving way in all things.

Deuteronomy 4:1, 5–9
Psalm 147
Matthew 5:17–19

# MARCH 31

*Listen to my voice; then I will be your God and you shall be my people. Walk in all the ways that I command you, so that you may prosper.*

—JEREMIAH 7:23

The breakthrough moment, whether in science or in prayer, often comes at the end of a long path of preparation. If we cut short the journey, we may miss the moment of truth.

Jeremiah 7:23–28
Psalm 95
Luke 11:14–23

# APRIL 1

*I will be like the dew for Israel:*
*he shall blossom like the lily;*
*He shall strike root like the Lebanon cedar,*
*and put forth his shoots.*

—HOSEA 14:6–7

Grace falls silently and seeps unnoticed into our hearts'
soil, yet its effects make the difference between futility
and fruitfulness.

Hosea 14:2–10
Psalm 81
Mark 12:28–34

*Come, let us return to the LORD,*
*For it is he who has rent, but he will heal us;*
*he has struck us, but he will bind our wounds.*
*He will revive us after two days;*
*on the third day he will raise us up,*
*to live in his presence.*

—HOSEA 6:1–2

The sharp blade of the farmer's plough sliced mercilessly through the weary wintering soil. The soil could not know that this was not an act of harming but of healing, and that as a direct result, there would be unimagined new growth in the spring.

Hosea 6:1–6
Psalm 51
Luke 18:9–14

*Sunday*

# APRIL 3

*Awake, O sleeper,*
*and arise from the dead,*
*and Christ will give you light.*

—EPHESIANS 5:14

Jane kept vigil all night at her sick child's bedside. When the child opened her eyes the next morning, she saw her mother's eyes gazing down upon her with infinite love. She never knew that this loving gaze had been resting upon her through the long hours of her fevered sleep. It was enough to rest in its warmth at the beginning of a new day.

1 Samuel 16:1, 6–7, 10–13
Psalm 23
Ephesians 5:8–14
John 9:1–41 or 9:1, 6–9, 13–17, 34–38

*Lo, I am about to create new heavens*
*and a new earth;*
*The things of the past shall not be remembered*
*or come to mind.*

—ISAIAH 65:17

There is an old tape player in my mind. It plays outdated
recordings over and over, leading me to make today's
choices under the shadow of what happened long ago. Like
the information on the hard drive of a discarded computer,
these data simply will not go away. Can I trust God's
promise to wipe it clean and set me free to live today in
newness of mind and heart and memory?

Isaiah 65:17–21
Psalm 30
John 4:43–54

# APRIL 5

• ST. VINCENT FERRER, PRIEST •

*One man was there who had been ill for thirty-eight years. When Jesus*
*saw him lying there and knew that he had been ill for a long time, he*
*said to him, "Do you want to be well?"*

—JOHN 5:5–6

To be sick may bring a subtle reward: others will be
sympathetic and help me; they won't expect too much
from me; they will pay attention to me. To be well may
bring renewed responsibilities: I'll have to resume my full
role at work, in the community, and in the family.

Let me look into my heart and give God my honest
answer. Do I truly want to be well? Do I truly want the
fullness of life that Jesus offers?

Ezekiel 47:1–9, 12
Psalm 46
John 5:1–16

*Wednesday*

# APRIL 6

*Can a mother forget her infant,*
*be without tenderness for the child of her womb?*
*Even should she forget,*
*I will never forget you.*

—ISAIAH 49:15

The mystery of our existence not only sustains our life but
also holds us in an intimacy of love beyond anything the
human mind can imagine.

Isaiah 49:8–15
Psalm 145
John 5:17–30

*Thursday*

# APRIL 7

• ST. JOHN BAPTIST DE LA SALLE, PRIEST •

*Ou fathers made a calf in Horeb*
*and adored a molten image;*
*They exchanged their glory*
*for the image of a grass-eating bullock.*
—PSALM 106:19–20

The grass-eating bull that we have established as the focus of our desire has migrated from Horeb to our twenty-first-century shopping malls and entertainment plazas, to our celebrity lineups and game shows. This bull grazes on our time and energy and credit cards, and it leaves us diminished and weary. It's a poor exchange for the living encounter with our glorious and loving Source.

Exodus 32:7–14
Psalm 106
John 5:31–47

*Some of the inhabitants of Jerusalem said, "Is he not the one they
are trying to kill? And look, he is speaking openly and they say
nothing to him."*

—JOHN 7:25

Clara wasn't about to put up with this arrogant young
intruder, who was burgling her home and threatening her
life. "What do you think your granny would have to say
to you if she could see you now?" she challenged him.
He stopped in his tracks; her words had sunk in. He had
nothing to say to her in response.

Sound unlikely? It really happened one day in a township
in South Africa!

Wisdom 2:1, 12–22
Psalm 34
John 7:1–2. 10, 25–30

# APRIL 9

*No prophet arises from Galilee.*
—JOHN 7:52

How neatly we have packaged our lives and mentally
organized people according to our own sets of expectations
and assumptions. And how completely God cuts through
our packaging to reveal just how spectacularly wrong
we can be.

Jeremiah 11:18–20
Psalm 7
John 7:40–53

# APRIL 10

*[Jesus] cried out in a loud voice, "Lazarus, come out!" The dead man came out, tied hand and foot with burial bands, and his face was wrapped in a cloth. So Jesus said to them, "Untie him and let him go."*

—JOHN 11:43–44

What dark and frightening imprisonment, perhaps of my own making, is Jesus inviting me to leave behind? From what bonds and limitations is he longing to liberate me?

How will I respond to his call to come out and be free?

Ezekiel 37:12–14
Psalm 130
Romans 8:8–11
John 11:1–45 or 11:3–7, 17, 20–27, 33–45

*[Jesus] straightened up and said to them, "Let the one among you who is
without sin be the first to throw a stone at her."*

—JOHN 8:7

The reproaches and destructive criticism we throw at one
another are very often not stones at all but boomerangs
that will come flying back at us with this message: "what
you so dislike in others is actually an aspect of yourself."

Daniel 13:1–9, 15–17, 19–30, 33–62 or 13:41–62
Psalm 23
John 8:1–11

*The LORD looked down from his holy height,*
*from heaven he beheld the earth,*
*To hear the groaning of the prisoners,*
*to release those doomed to die.*

—PSALM 102:20–21

The spirit of compassion means nothing at all if it does not come close enough to another troubled heart to listen, to liberate, and to love.

Numbers 21:4–9
Psalm 102
John 8:21–30

*I see four men unfettered and unhurt, walking in the fire, and the fourth looks like a son of God.*

—DANIEL 3:92

Sometimes we glimpse a deeper peace in the heat of the conflict; a still center in the eye of the storm; a silent, invisible presence alongside us when we most need but least expect it. When this happens, we are meeting God-with-us, which dissolves doubt in moments of absolute trust.

Daniel 3:14–20, 91–92, 95
Daniel 3:52–56
John 8:31–42

*Amen, amen, I say to you, before Abraham came to be, I AM.*

—JOHN 8:58

Sometimes I experience something—a story, a flash of insight, a moment of clarity—and I know that I always knew it but never knew that I knew it. When this happens, I know that the eternal Presence has fleetingly touched my own present moment.

Genesis 17:3–9
Psalm 105
John 8:51–59

*In my distress I called upon the LORD*
*and cried out to my God;*
*From his temple he heard my voice,*
*and my cry to him reached his ears.*

—PSALM 18:7

At a time of crisis in my life I remember finding no words
with which to pray except the Taizé chant: "O Lord, hear
my prayer . . . come and listen to me." I prayed it over and
over. It took years before I could look back and see how
the help I begged for had been given—how surely and
how wisely, but in God's time, not mine.

Jeremiah 20:10–13
Psalm 18
John 10:31–42

*I will turn their mourning into joy,*
*I will console and gladden them after their sorrows.*
—JEREMIAH 31:13

As we stand on the threshold of Jesus' darkest days, we are reminded that joy lives on the other side of mourning and gladness on the other side of grief. The promise is true. The way is clear. There is no bypass—no alternative, more scenic route.

Dare we enter the darkness and trust that it is indeed a gateway to light?

Ezekiel 37:21–28
Jeremiah 31:10–13
John 11:45–56

# APRIL 17

• PALM SUNDAY OF THE LORD'S PASSION •

*Behold, your king comes to you,*
*meek and riding on an ass,*
*and on a colt, the foal of a beast of burden.*

—MATTHEW 21:5

The humblest, least regarded of creatures carries the One
who reveals to us the face of God. Very often it is the
humblest and least regarded of our sisters and brothers
who most vividly reflect the presence of God in our midst.

Matthew 21:1–11
Isaiah 50:4–7
Psalm 22
Philippians 2:6–11
Matthew 26:14—27:66 or 27:11–54

# APRIL 18

*Mary took a liter of costly perfumed oil made from genuine aromatic nard and anointed the feet of Jesus and dried them with her hair; the house was filled with the fragrance of the oil.*

—JOHN 12:3

Maureen worked in a hospice. Everyone who knew her said that wherever she was, ministering to those on the brink of death, touching them with love, the whole room seemed to glow with warmth that flowed from her quiet compassion.

Isaiah 42:1–7
Psalm 27
John 12:1–11

*Jesus was deeply troubled and testified, "Amen, amen, I say to you, one of you will betray me."*

—JOHN 13:21

Jesus is betrayed by one from his innermost circle, one who breaks bread with him. Perhaps we would also like to think of ourselves as belonging to his innermost circle. Perhaps we are also eager to dip our hands into the bowl at his table.

And perhaps we also betray him in a thousand ways each day, even as we convince ourselves that we are acting for the best.

Isaiah 49:1–6
Psalm 71
John 13:21–33, 36–38

*Go into the city to a certain man and tell him, "The teacher says, 'My appointed time draws near; in your house I shall celebrate the Passover with my disciples.'"*

—MATTHEW 26:18

No longer is this a house in ancient Jerusalem, but your house and my house. This man, about to be executed as a threat to national security, is dining with us tonight. Will we take courage and, in faith, open our door to him?

Isaiah 50:4–9
Psalm 69
Matthew 26:14–25

*This is my body that is for you. Do this in remembrance of me.*
—1 CORINTHIANS 11:24

Through all the complications we have constructed around Eucharist, can we still hear Jesus' challenge: "Are you willing to let your life be spent for the sake of others? Are you willing to pour out your life's energy in the service of the whole human family? This is what I ask that you do in remembrance of me."

**Chrism Mass:**
Isaiah 61:1–3, 6, 8–9
Psalm 89
Revelation 1:5–8
Luke 4:16–21

**Evening Mass of the Lord's Supper:**
Exodus 12:1–8, 11–14
Psalm 116
1 Corinthians 11:23–26
John 13:1–15

*Friday*

# APRIL 22

*He grew up like a sapling before him,*
*like a shoot from the parched earth;*
*There was in him no stately bearing to make us look at him,*
*nor appearance that would attract us to him.*
*He was spurned and avoided by people,*
*a man of suffering, accustomed to infirmity,*
*One of those from whom people hide their faces.*

—ISAIAH 53:2–3

Every time I recoil from the ugliness of the world or shield my eyes against the twisted faces of those whom this world has hurt, let me remember that in these very people I am encountering the man of sorrows.

Isaiah 52:13—53:12
Psalm 31
Hebrews 4:14–16, 5:7–9
John 18:1—19:42

───────────

*And behold, Jesus met [the women] on their way and greeted them.*
*They approached, embraced his feet, and did him homage. Then Jesus*
*said to them, "Do not be afraid. Go tell my brothers to go to Galilee,*
*and there they will see me."*

—MATTHEW 28:9–10

After the world-shattering events in Jerusalem, Jesus sends
his friends back to Galilee, where it all began. Perhaps he
says to us as well, "However far you travel in search of me,
you will find my risen presence back home in your own
heart, and your own life's circumstances."

Genesis 1:1—2:2 or 1:1, 26–31
Psalm 104 or 33
Genesis 22:1–18 or 22:1–2, 9a, 10–13,
15–18
Psalm 16
Exodus 14:15—15:1
Exodus 15:1–6, 17–18
Isaiah 54:5–14
Psalm 30

Isaiah 55:1–11
Isaiah 12:2–6
Baruch 3:9–15, 32—4:4
Psalm 19
Ezekiel 36:16–17a, 18–28
Psalm 42/43 or Isaiah 12:2–6 or Psalm 51
Romans 6:3–11
Psalm 118
Matthew 28:1–10

*Sunday*

# APRIL 24

• EASTER SUNDAY * THE RESURRECTION OF THE LORD •

*When Simon Peter arrived after him, he went into the tomb and saw the burial cloths there, and the cloth that had covered his head, not with the burial cloths but rolled up in a separate place.*

—JOHN 20:6–7

Jesus gently leaves behind the outer wrappings of his mortal life to be free to embrace the new. May God grant us the same freedom to leave the past behind without reproach or regret when it is time for us to move on to new dimensions of life.

Acts 10:34, 37–43
Psalm 118
Colossians 3:1–4 or 1 Corinthians 5:6–8
John 20:1–9 or Matthew 28:1–10 or Luke 24:13–35

*Monday*

# APRIL 25

• ST. MARK, EVANGELIST •

*I set the LORD ever before me;*
*with him at my right hand I shall not be disturbed.*
*Therefore my heart is glad and my soul rejoices,*
*my body, too, abides in confidence.*

—PSALM 16:8–9

On the few occasions when I really knew that, in spite of myself, I was following a path that felt really right, I also discovered that there seemed to be wings on my heels and every obstacle slid aside to let me pass. My way became a journey of joy.

Acts 2:14, 22–33
Psalm 16
Matthew 28:8–15

# APRIL 26

*Jesus said to her, "Mary!" She turned and said to him in Hebrew, "Rabbouni," which means Teacher.*

—JOHN 20:16

A simple exchange of names, a personal exchange, a heart-to-heart interaction. It was all Mary needed to open her eyes to the miracle of life calling her forward. The Creator of the Universe speaks person to person.

Acts 2:36–41
Psalm 33
John 20:11–18

*Wednesday*

# APRIL 27

*They said to each other, "Were not our hearts burning within us while*
*he spoke to us on the way and opened the Scriptures to us?"*
—LUKE 24:32

It was a fire that would set the world alight as it took hold
of human hearts. Like the Olympic flame, it still passes
from hand to hand, heart to heart, life to life. In our time
and our place it now rests in our care.

Acts 3:1–10
Psalm 105
Luke 24:13–35

# APRIL 28

*While they were still speaking about this, he stood in their midst and
said to them, "Peace be with you."*
—LUKE 24:36

The Scots call it "blether" when people get tangled up in
a torrent of words as they try to work things out. Jesus
cuts right through the blether with the simple gift of his
presence and his peace.

Acts 3:11–26
Psalm 8
Luke 24:35–48

*When it was already dawn, Jesus was standing on the shore; but the disciples did not realize that it was Jesus. Jesus said to them, "Children, have you caught anything to eat?" They answered him, "No." So he said to them, "Cast the net over the right side of the boat and you will find something."*

—JOHN 21:4–6

Sometimes just a very small shift from port to starboard—from one point of view to another—is enough to move us from futility to fruitfulness. But to embrace this possibility we will have to listen very carefully to the wisdom of the one who stands on the shore.

Acts 4:1–12
Psalm 118
John 21:1–14

*[Mary Magdalene] went and told his companions who were mourning and weeping. When they heard that he was alive and had been seen by her, they did not believe.*

—MARK 16:10–11

Are the tears we shed for the grief, pain, and losses of the past blinding us to the future that God is holding out to us? In such circumstances does our faith shrink into disbelief?

Acts 4:13–21
Psalm 118
Mark 16:9–15

*On the evening of that first day of the week, when the doors were locked, where the disciples were, for fear of the Jews, Jesus came and stood in their midst and said to them, "Peace be with you."*

—JOHN 20:19–20

We are quite the experts when it comes to doors. We know how to make doors of prejudice, fear, denial, exclusion, defense—the list is endless. Jesus ignores all the keep out! signs and walks right in, bringing one gift only: peace!

Acts 2:42–47
Psalm 118
1 Peter 1:3–9
John 20:19–31

*Monday*

# MAY 2

*The wind blows where it wills, and you can hear the sound it makes, but you do not know where it comes from or where it goes; so it is with everyone who is born of the Spirit.*

—JOHN 3:8

We have created whole books of maps of where the Spirit is supposed to flow, through the channels we have set up for God's convenience. But the Spirit doesn't read our maps. May the Spirit always continue to take us utterly by surprise, wherever the Spirit chooses to be manifest.

Acts 4:23–31
Psalm 2
John 3:1–8

*Tuesday*

# MAY 3

• ST. PHILIP AND ST. JAMES, APOSTLES •

*After that, he appeared to more than five hundred brothers and sisters at once, most of whom are still living, though some have fallen asleep. After that he appeared to James, then to all the Apostles. Last of all, as to one born abnormally, he appeared to me.*

—1 CORINTHIANS 15:6–7

We are familiar with the stories of the risen Lord appearing to his followers, making them living witnesses to the Resurrection. But Paul's testimony might touch our own experience. Maybe we didn't experience visions as the first apostles did, but still we are witnesses to the Resurrection. Take a moment to remember times when you, too, have been utterly convinced of the power of the risen Jesus because it has broken forth in some personal way in your own life, bringing you to new growth and empowerment.

1 Corinthians 15:1–8
Psalm 19
John 14:6–14

# MAY 4

*For God did not send his Son into the world to condemn the world, but that the world might be saved through him.*

—JOHN 3:17

In the light of this promise, it might be good to pause for a while today and reflect on what kind of image we hold of God. Is God a police officer or stern teacher waiting to catch us in a wrongdoing or an omnipotent judge with the power to send us into eternal night?

John says, "No!" God reveals, through Jesus, that God's overwhelming desire is to bring us to the fullness of everything we can become.

Acts 5:17–26
Psalm 34
John 3:16–21

*We must obey God rather then men. The God of our ancestors raised Jesus, though you had him killed by hanging him on a tree.*

—ACTS 5:29–30

God is not opposed to us—when we obey the command of God we will continuously strive for the very best for the men, women, and children whose lives interact with our own. But sometimes obeying God means that we can't let a human relationship overshadow or diminish our central relationship with God.

Acts 5:27–33
Psalm 34
John 3:31–36

*Friday*
# MAY 6

*So now I tell you, have nothing to do with these men, and let them go.*
*For if this endeavor or this activity is of human origin, it will destroy*
*itself. But if it comes from God, you will not be able to destroy them;*
*you may even find yourselves fighting against God.*

—ACTS 5:38–39

I have noticed that when an idea or a project is truly
inspired by the Spirit it takes flight and moves forward on
its own energy, with minimal help from me! If it is just my
own idea, however hard I might work at it, it often runs
into the ground and comes to nothing.

Acts 5:34–42
Psalm 27
John 6:1–15

⇒ 160 ⇐

*The sea was stirred up because a strong wind was blowing. When they had rowed about three or four miles, they saw Jesus walking on the sea and coming near the boat, and they began to be afraid.*

—JOHN 6:18–19

Life is giving me a rough ride. I'm miles away from my comfort zone. The wind is rising, and the seas are high. It might be that, at precisely that moment, I get a glimpse, a touch, a whisper of a presence close by that I never expected and don't understand. It scares and consoles me at the same time. I know it is you, Lord. Touch my chaos with your calm.

Acts 6:1–7
Psalm 33
John 6:16–21

*And it happened that, while he was with them at table, he took bread, said the blessing, broke it, and gave it to them. With that their eyes were opened and they recognized him, but he vanished from their sight.*

—LUKE 24:30–31

Once I have experienced a familiar gesture in a life-transforming moment, it is imprinted indelibly on my soul. If I see it again, it sparks a sacred memory and opens my eyes to recognize what I have once known and can never forget.

Acts 2:14, 22–33
Psalm 16
1 Peter 1:17–21
Luke 24:13–35

*Do not work for food that perishes but for the food that endures for eternal life, which the Son of Man will give you.*

—JOHN 6:27

One of the saddest sights is that of a deceased person's house being cleaned out. He accumulated so much over the years, but what really mattered about this person's life? Ask those who knew him. Ask about how he added zest and joy to the neighborhood, how he infused integrity into the workplace, and how he was always there when his grandchildren needed him.

Acts 6:8–15
Psalm 119
John 6:22–29

*I am the bread of life; whoever comes to me will never hunger, and whoever believes in me will never thirst.*

—JOHN 6:35

It doesn't get more ordinary than bread and water: basic, daily essentials. If I really believe in Jesus' words, then my relationship with him is also meant to be an everyday matter, a basic essential for living and growing.

Acts 7:51—8:1
Psalm 31
John 6:30–35

*Wednesday*
# MAY 11

*I will not reject anyone who comes to me.*

—JOHN 6:37

This is the One we follow: the One who never turns
anyone away from his table, whether or not they fit in,
whether or not they have kept the rules. How could we
treat people otherwise?

Acts 8:1–8
Psalm 66
John 6:35–40

*Thursday*

# MAY 12

*Your ancestors ate the manna in the desert, but they died; this is the bread that comes down from heaven so that one may eat it and not die.*

—JOHN 6:49–50

Like caterpillars, we munch our way through the good things our consumer society offers, getting fatter every day. And then we die.

Jesus tells us that it isn't about being a fatter caterpillar but about letting go and becoming a butterfly.

Acts 8:26–40
Psalm 66
John 6:44–51

*Saul got up from the ground, but when he opened his eyes he could see nothing; so they led him by the hand and brought him to Damascus.*

—ACTS 9:8

When God moves in on my life, the things I thought I could see so clearly suddenly seem dim. The control I thought I had must be surrendered to God's guiding. Only then will my lost sight become insight and my self-assurance turn into faith.

Acts 9:1–20
Psalm 117
John 6:52–59

*"Therefore, it is necessary that one of the men who accompanied us the whole time the Lord Jesus came and went among us, beginning from the baptism of John until the day on which he was taken up from us, become with us a witness to his resurrection." . . . [A]nd the lot fell upon Matthias, and he was counted with the Eleven Apostles.*

—ACTS 1: 21–22, 26

The apostles are looking to replace Judas. This new apostle must know Jesus personally, not just know about him; must have entered into the events of Jesus' life and made them the core of their own life; must know that the power of the risen Lord is active in the here and now. Imagine that the lot falls to you. How will you respond? God is commissioning new apostles all the time to go out and share the Good News.

Acts 1:15–17, 20–26
Psalm 113
John 15:9–17

*Sunday*

# MAY 15

• FOURTH SUNDAY OF EASTER •

*I am the gate. Whoever enters through me will be saved, and will come in and go out and find pasture.*

—JOHN 10:9

A gate offers this silent message: "when you think there is no way forward, a new possibility opens up." A gate is always an invitation to move to the new pasture and to be free. Jesus is the invitation to come into our true home and true selves.

Acts 2:14, 36–41
Psalm 23
1 Peter 2:20–25
John 10:1–10

*I have other sheep that do not belong to this fold. These also I must lead, and they will hear my voice, and there will be one flock, one shepherd.*

—JOHN 10:16

The "other sheep" are all around us: the people we don't like or don't agree with, the people who criticize us or show up our weaknesses, the people we envy or resent or try to ignore. They belong to God's flock as surely as we do.

Acts 11:1–18
Psalms 42, 43
John 10:11–18

*The Jews gathered around him and said to him, "How long are you going to keep us in suspense? If you are the Messiah, tell us plainly." Jesus answered them, "I told you and you do not believe. The works I do in my Father's name testify to me."*

—JOHN 10:24–25

Where is Christ today? How we might wish we could see him plainly! Yet his words are just as valid and relevant today as when he first spoke them. He says even now, "Look for the hands that do my work today, the eyes that see as I saw, and the hearts that love others in the way I love. Then you will see where I am."

Acts 11:19–26
Psalm 87
John 10:22–30

*I came into the world as light, so that everyone who believes in me might
not remain in darkness.*

—JOHN 12:46

Little Kathy woke up screaming in the night. Her parents
rushed to her room, switched on her bedside light, and
comforted her. The light and their love had instantly
banished the nightmare, and she was at peace again.

Acts 12:24—13:5
Psalm 67
John 12:44—50

*Thursday*

# MAY 19

*Amen, amen, I say to you, whoever receives the one I send receives me,*
*and whoever receives me receives the one who sent me.*

—JOHN 13:20

We have no problem in welcoming you, Lord—we do it in
style every Sunday. But who are these Monday-to-Saturday
people that you're sending? We never noticed them. Are
we missing something?

Acts 13:13–25
Psalm 89
John 13:16–20

*In my Father's house there are many dwelling places. If there were not, would I have told you that I am going to prepare a place for you?*
—JOHN 14:2

We may well be surprised at some of the people we meet in heaven. But not as surprised, perhaps, as they will be to see us.

Acts 13:26–33
Psalm 2
John 14:1–6

*If you know me, then you will also know my Father. From now on you do know him and have seen him. . . . Whoever has seen me has seen the Father.*

—JOHN 14:7, 9

When our hearts and minds are conformed to the mind and heart of Christ, then we will see the whole world in a grain of sand. And we'll see the Creator of that world in one another's eyes.

Acts 13:44–52
Psalm 98
John 14:7–14

*Behold, I am laying a stone in Zion,*
*a cornerstone, chosen and precious,*
*and whoever believes in it shall not be put to shame.*

—1 PETER 2:6

A wise friend once said to me, "When you are trying to decide between A and B, sometimes X is the answer." Jesus is an X, the cornerstone who holds our oppositions in balance and builds our disconnections into a new unity and integrity.

Acts 6:1–7
Psalm 33
1 Peter 2:4–9
John 14:1–12

*Monday*

# MAY 23

*Whoever loves me will keep my word, and my Father will love him, and we will come to him and make our dwelling with him.*

—JOHN 14:23

It's natural for those who love each other to want to make a home together.

God is waiting. I need only to say the word.

Acts 14:5–18
Psalm 115
John 14:21–26

*Peace I leave with you; my peace I give to you. Not as the world gives do I give it to you.*

—JOHN 14:27

In some families peace means avoiding any topic of conversation that might start an argument. In others, peace means not talking at all. In God's family, peace means an all-embracing attitude of love in which anything can be said without fear of judgment and in which everyone is respected and valued. This kind of loving makes war obsolete.

Acts 14:19–28
Psalm 145
John 14:27–31

• ST. BEDE THE VENERABLE, PRIEST AND DOCTOR OF THE CHURCH •
ST. GREGORY VII, POPE & ST. MARY MAGDALENE DE 'PAZZI, VIRGIN •

*I am the vine, you are the branches. Whoever remains in me and I in
him will bear much fruit, because without me you can do nothing.*

—JOHN 15:5

Jim had a plum tree that bore loads of fruit every year. Jim
made certain it received the water and other nourishment
it needed, and he pruned the branches to keep it healthy.
But one summer lightning struck a large branch toward the
top of the tree, and there it hung, broken and dangling.
When the fruit came that year, the broken branch was
conspicuously bare. Although still attached by the tough
bark, that branch could no longer draw life from the tree
itself. The plums that had begun to form merely shriveled
and dried before developing fully.

Acts 15:1–6
Psalm 122
John 15:1–8

*Thursday*

# MAY 26

• ST. PHILIP NERI, PRIEST •

*If you keep my commandments, you will remain in my love, just as I have kept my Father's commandments and remain in his love.*

—JOHN 15:10

In the garden there was a beautiful fishpond. Most of the fish were content to glide around in the sun-warmed water, but one of them had an independent streak and managed to flip itself out of the water and onto a stone. Very soon that fish was dead. It had removed itself from the source of life.

Acts 15:7–21
Psalm 96
John 15:9–11

---

*It was not you who chose me, but I who chose you and appointed you
to go and bear fruit that will remain, so that whatever you ask the
Father in my name he may give you.*

—JOHN 15:16

Sue had moved to a new town, where she knew no one.
After searching around for a church community she liked,
she became frustrated and increasingly lonely. Nothing
felt right. She didn't know which to choose, if any. Then
a neighbor knocked on her door one morning with some
flowers and a loaf of freshly baked bread. "Come and have
coffee with us." Sue's loneliness ebbed. She knew she had
been chosen, singled out for love by this kind stranger.

"Thank you," she said. "Thank you so much."

Acts 15:22–31
Psalm 57
John 15:12–17

*If the world hates you, realize that it hated me first. If you belonged to the world, the world would love its own; but because you do not belong to the world, and I have chosen you out of the world, the world hates you.*

—JOHN 15:18–19

Wherever we listen to the voice of truth and integrity within us, and act on what we hear, we will provoke the shadow side of humankind and bring hostility down upon us.

Acts 16:1–10
Psalm 100
John 15:18–21

*For it is better to suffer for doing good, if that be the will of God, than for doing evil.*

—1 PETER 3:17

An elderly aunt who knew nothing of theology used to tell me, "It's better to suffer injustice than to act unjustly." As a child I didn't understand what she meant, but as I have gone through life, I've often thought back to her wisdom and tried to let it guide my choices.

Acts 8:5–8, 14–17
Psalm 66
1 Peter 3:15–18
John 14:15–21

_Monday_

# MAY 30

*They will expel you from the synagogues; in fact, the hour is coming*
*when everyone who kills you will think he is offering worship to God.*

—JOHN 16:2

God must surely weep constant tears over the violence
that is carried out in God's name. How easy it is to
deceive ourselves into thinking that what we do is God's
will. But our various causes blind us to the one overriding
command: "Love God and your neighbor."

Acts 16:11–15
Psalm 149
John 15:26—16:4

⇒ 184 ⇐

• THE VISITATION OF THE VIRGIN MARY TO ELIZABETH •

*At the moment the sound of your greeting reached my ears, the infant in my womb leaped for joy. Blessed are you who believed that what was spoken to you by the Lord would be fulfilled.*

—LUKE 1:44–45

Whenever two human hearts who are one in Christ meet together, the Christ who is coming to birth within each of them leaps in recognition of the Christ coming to birth in the other. The leap of joy is a blessing of hope that the promise of God is already an incarnate reality in our lives and in our world even though we cannot yet perceive its fullness.

Zephaniah 3:14–18 or Romans 12:9–16
Isaiah 12:2–6
Luke 1:39–56

*Wednesday*

# JUNE 1

• ST. JUSTIN, MARTYR •

*As I walked around looking carefully at your shrines, I even discovered an altar inscribed, "To an Unknown God." What therefore you unknowingly worship, I proclaim to you.*

—ACTS 17:23

In the heart of every atheist is a sacred core in which the unknown God is at home. Let us remember this, before we judge. And then let us suspend judgment.

Acts 17:15, 22—18:1
Psalm 148
John 16:12–15

*May the God of our Lord Jesus Christ, the Father of glory, give you a Spirit of wisdom and revelation resulting in knowledge of him. May the eyes of your hearts be enlightened, that you may know what is the hope that belongs to his call.*

—EPHESIANS 1:17–18

On this day we celebrate that Jesus ascended into heaven to sit at the right hand of God the Father. But we, too, are energized by that power—in all that we do and say in this existence we know as God's "kingdom" here and now. Through our prayers, our praise, and our hopes, we ascend daily into God's loving presence.

Acts 1:1–11
Psalm 47
Ephesians 1:17–23
Matthew 28:16–20

*When a woman is in labor, she is in anguish because her hour
has arrived; but when she has given birth to a child, she no longer
remembers the pain because of her joy that a child has been born
into the world.*

—JOHN 16:21

When I look back to my daughter's birth, my head knows
that it was painful, but my heart, truly, remembers only
the joy, which was so much greater than the pain. One
day I believe that, perhaps from eternity, I will look back
over the painful parts of my life and they, too, will be
completely superseded by all that has brought joy, growth,
and new life.

Acts 18:9–18
Psalm 47
John 16:20–23

# JUNE 4

*For king of all the earth is God;*
*sing hymns of praise.*
*God reigns over the nations,*
*God sits upon his holy throne.*
— PSALM 47:8–9

Just as a toy magnet is, itself, subject to the magnetic force of the earth's gravity, so too our man-made power systems are subject to God—whether or not they realize it.

Acts 18:23–28
Psalm 47
John 16:23–28

*I pray for them. I do not pray for the world but for the ones you have given me, because they are yours.*

—JOHN 17:9

During stressful times, we often feel the upholding power of one another's prayers. How much more powerful, then, is this prayer, uttered for each of us two thousand years ago. Jesus' prayer for us continues to reverberate through time and space, from the One whose love holds us eternally.

Acts 1:12–14
Psalm 27
1 Peter 4:13–16
John 17: 1–11

# JUNE 6

*The father of orphans and the defender of widows*
*is God in his holy dwelling.*
*God gives a home to the forsaken;*
*he leads forth prisoners to prosperity.*

—PSALM 68:6–7

God walks our streets today, disguised as the social
worker, finding a foster home for an abandoned child.
God is the young person working at the homeless shelter,
the Alcoholics Anonymous mentor walking alongside the
recovering alcoholic, the attorney taking pro bono cases on
behalf of the dispossessed. Let us greet God when we meet
God, and may we add our efforts to God's unceasing work.

Acts 19:1–8
Psalm 68
John 16:29–33

*A bountiful rain you showered down, O God, upon your inheritance;*
*you restored the land when it languished;*
*Your flock settled in it;*
*in your goodness, O God, you provided it for the needy.*
—PSALM 68:10–11

Jason has never forgotten the days when he was homeless
and the kindness of some of the people he encountered.
A few dollars would mean another meal, another day's
survival. But the truly generous rain came down for him
when someone would stop to share a few words, a little
time, a spark of love with him. Those were life saving. Such
kindness reminded him that he was still a human being. It
was manna for his soul.

Acts 20:17–27
Psalm 68
John 17:1–11

# JUNE 8

*It is more blessed to give than to receive.*

—ACTS 20:35

If you want to see something more wonderful than even a
child's expression as she unwraps the gift you have given
her, notice the overflowing joy in her eyes as she watches,
breath held, as you unwrap the gift she has made for you.

Acts 20:28–38
Psalm 68
John 17:11–19

*I made known to them your name and I will make it known, that the love with which you loved me may be in them and I in them.*

—JOHN 17:26

Jesus makes this prayer shortly before his death. His promise to continue to make God known to God's people passes into our hands, through the undying power of the Spirit. Have we truly accepted this legacy and acted upon it?

Acts 22:30, 23:6–11
Psalm 16
John 17:20–26

*When you were younger, you used to dress yourself and go where you wanted; but when you grow old, you will stretch out your hands, and someone else will dress you and lead you where you do not want to go.*

—JOHN 21:18

"Old Mrs. Jenkins is cranky and difficult today," complained the young nurse.

"No," said her supervisor. "She is fearful and anxious because she no longer has any control over what happens to her. Walk a loving mile with her, and you will notice a difference."

Acts 25:13–21
Psalm 103
John 21:15–19

*When he arrived and saw the grace of God, he rejoiced and encouraged
them all to remain faithful to the Lord in firmness of heart, for he was a
good man, filled with the holy Spirit and faith.*

—ACTS 11:23–24

Isn't it interesting what we learn about Barnabas from
these few words? He recognized God's grace at work; he
was joyful; and he encouraged others. All of this because
he was filled with the Holy Spirit. Being a "good" man or
woman isn't so complicated after all.

Acts 11:21–26; 13:1–3
Psalm 98
John 21:20–25

*If you take away their breath, they perish*
*and return to their dust.*
*When you send forth your spirit, they are created,*
*and you renew the face of the earth.*

—PSALM 104:29–30

In my kitchen, where I see it every day, I've placed a little twig
from a shrub called the rose of Jericho. It looks dried and
shriveled, but if I simply hold it under running water and give
it a little drink, it opens and becomes fresh and green. When I
neglect it, it folds in on itself and waits until I remember it, but
it doesn't die. When I remember it, it opens to me with new
and verdant life. It reminds me every morning that without
God's Spirit I am nothing; with it I am fully alive.

**Vigil:**
Genesis 11:1–9 or Exodus 19:3–8, 16–20,
or Ezekiel 37:1–14 or Joel 3:1–5
Psalm 104
Romans 8:22–27
John 7:37–39

**Mass:**
Acts 2:1–11
Psalm 104
1 Corinthians 12:3–7, 12–13
John 20:19–23

*[We are treated] as dying and behold we live; as chastised and yet not put to death; as sorrowful yet always rejoicing.*

—2 CORINTHIANS 6:9–10

The newspapers tell us every day how bad things are.
The Gospel speaks of hope and renewal.
The television newscasts would have us all dead
and buried.
The Gospel announces transformation.
Which are we going to believe?

2 Corinthians 6:1–10
Psalm 98
Matthew 5:38–42

# JUNE 14

*You have heard that it was said, "You shall love your neighbor and hate your enemy." But I say to you, love your enemies, and pray for those who persecute you.*

—MATTHEW 5:43–44

Jesus' words throw common sense overboard and turn our expectations upside down. He warns that competition must give way to cooperation, individual gain to mutual well-being, clenched fist and raised hand to a listening ear and an understanding heart. Perhaps that is the only way we will survive as a human family on this planet.

2 Corinthians 8:1–9
Psalm 146
Matthew 5:43–48

*Wednesday*

# JUNE 15

*Consider this: whoever sows sparingly will also reap sparingly, and whoever sows bountifully will also reap bountifully. Each must do as already determined, without sadness or compulsion, for God loves a cheerful giver.*

—2 CORINTHIANS 9:6–7

Jamie always put the minimum effort into all he did. He skimped on his schoolwork and failed his exams. He neglected his partner and lost his family. He took the line of least resistance, and it led him to unhappiness.

His brother John was very different. He gave everything his best shot. He worked at his marriage, spent time with his children, and lived generously in his community. His life path cost effort, but it led him, and others, to joy.

2 Corinthians 9:6–11
Psalm 112
Matthew 6:1–6, 16–18

*In praying, do not babble like the pagans, who think that they will be heard because of their many words. Do not be like them. Your Father knows what you need before you ask him.*

—MATTHEW 6:7–8

A spoonful of silence is worth a waterfall of words. Within it we are invited to see ourselves and one another as we truly are, stripped of all the verbs, nouns, and adjectives.

2 Corinthians 11:1–11
Psalm 111
Matthew 6:7–15

*Do not store up for yourselves treasures on earth, where moth and decay destroy, and thieves break in and steal.*

—MATTHEW 6:19

Recession may slice through my savings,
inflation may swallow my pension,
crashing markets may take my job and repossess my
mortgaged home.
But nothing on earth can steal my hope,
or undermine my faith,
or obliterate my love,
without my permission.

2 Corinthians 11:18, 21–30
Psalm 34
Matthew 6:19–23

# JUNE 18

*My grace is sufficient for you, for power is made perfect in weakness.*

—2 CORINTHIANS 12:9

The best thing I can offer God is empty, receptive space, because that makes the least resistance to the flow of the Spirit. My strength, real or imagined, can block that flow. My weakness gives it free passage.

2 Corinthians 12:1–10
Psalm 34
Matthew 6:24–34

*Sunday*

# JUNE 19

*The grace of the Lord Jesus Christ and the love of God and the*
*fellowship of the Holy Spirit be with all of you.*
—2 CORINTHIANS 13:13

When we link hands and pray these words, we are actually passing on to one another the free gifting that Jesus reveals. We are promising to love one another with the wholly unearned love that flows from God. And we are acknowledging that we are in an unbreakable relationship with all that exists.

Exodus 34:4–6, 8–9
Daniel 3:52–55
2 Corinthians 13:11–13
John 3:16–18

*Stop judging, that you may not be judged. For as you judge, so will you be judged, and the measure with which you measure will be measured out to you.*

—MATTHEW 7:1–2

Native American wisdom warns us never to judge others until we have walked a mile in their moccasins. If we try to do that, we will discover that no one else's moccasins quite fit our feet, and our moccasins don't fit theirs. To discover that each of us has unique circumstances, personality traits, and reactions is a great first step toward learning not to judge.

Genesis 12:1–9
Psalm 33
Matthew 7:1–5

*Tuesday*

# JUNE 21

*Do not give what is holy to dogs, or throw your pearls before swine, lest they trample them underfoot, and turn and tear you to pieces.*

—MATTHEW 7:6

Pearls are formed in pain, as oysters shield their innermost parts from the lacerations of alien grains of grit. The pearls of our sacred journey are likewise often shaped in pain. Let them not be shared lightly with those who do not understand their holiness.

Genesis 13:2, 5–18
Psalm 15
Matthew 7:6, 12–14

• ST. PAULINAS OF NOLA, BISHOP • ST. JOHN FISHER, BISHOP AND MARTYR • ST. THOMAS MORE, MARTYR •

*He remembers forever his covenant*
*which he made binding for a thousand generations—*
*Which he entered into with Abraham*
*and by his oath to Isaac.*

—PSALM 105:8–9

How hard it is for us to commit ourselves to another person even for a week, let alone for a lifetime. A commitment for all eternity is beyond our comprehension. Only God could make such a promise.

Genesis 15:1–12, 17–18
Psalm 105
Matthew 7:15–20

*Everyone who listens to these words of mine and acts on them will be like a wise man who built his house on rock. The rain fell, the floods came, and the winds blew and buffeted the house. But it did not collapse; it had been set solidly on rock.*

—MATTHEW 7:24–25

The waves are pounding along the beach. A child is building a sand castle. A seagull is perched on a rock. Soon the incoming tide will flood the shore and all the sand castles will have been swept away. But tomorrow the seagull will still be able to perch on the rock. What aspects of our own lives will be swept away as soon as hard times come? Our status and self-importance? Even our physical health? And where is the solid rock? Our loving relationships, our desire to make a difference. Our faith.

Genesis 16:1–12, 15–16 or 16:6–12, 15–16
Psalm 106
Matthew 7:21–29

*Friday*

# JUNE 24

*When they came on the eighth day to circumcise the child, they were*
*going to call him Zechariah after his father, but his mother said in reply,*
*"No. He will be called John." But they answered her, "There is no one*
*among your relatives who has this name." So they made signs, asking*
*his father what he wished him to be called. He asked for a tablet and*
*wrote, "John is his name," and all were amazed. Immediately his mouth*
*was opened, his tongue freed, and he spoke blessing God.*

—LUKE 1:59–64

Imagine the stir this little scene created. The baby is to
have a name that is totally new—a break from all that has
gone before, just as John himself will lead the people to
a totally new threshold in the experience of God as he
heralds the arrival of Jesus. Zechariah will be the father of
the one who speaks a new word into the human wilderness.

| **Vigil:** | **Day:** |
|:---:|:---:|
| Jeremiah 1:4–10 | Isaiah 49:1–6 |
| Psalm 71 | Psalm 139 |
| 1 Peter 1:8–12 | Acts 13:22–26 |
| Luke 1:5–17 | Luke 1:57–66, 80 |

*When Jesus entered Capernaum, a centurion approached him and appealed to him, saying, "Lord, my servant is lying at home paralyzed, suffering dreadfully." He said to him, "I will come and cure him." The centurion said in reply, "Lord, I am not worthy to have you enter under my roof; only say the word and my servant will be healed."*

—MATTHEW 8:5–8

The centurion is the first of many who will come to trust that the Lord's word is all that is needed to bring new energy to their paralyzed lives.

Genesis 18:1–15
Luke 1:46–50, 53–55
Matthew 8:5–17

*The cup of blessing that we bless, is it not a participation in the blood of Christ? The bread that we break, is it not a participation in the body of Christ?*

—1 CORINTHIANS 10:16

We are the Body of Christ in our own time and place. To share in the breaking of the communion bread is to express our readiness to walk the path that Jesus walked, wherever it may lead. When we make our communion, we are making a commitment to become a living expression, in our own circumstances, of what we are receiving.

Deuteronomy 8:2–3, 14–16
Psalm 147
1 Corinthians 10:16–17
John 6:51–58

*Foxes have dens and birds of the sky have nests, but the Son of Man has nowhere to rest his head.*

—MATTHEW 8:20

When we follow the One who is the Way, then the journey itself becomes our home.

Genesis 18:16–33
Psalm 103
Matthew 8:18–22

*The sun was just rising over the earth as Lot arrived in Zoar; at the same time the LORD rained down sulphurous fire upon Sodom and Gomorrah from the LORD out of heaven. He overthrew those cities and the whole Plain, together with the inhabitants of the cities and the produce of the soil. But Lot's wife looked back, and she was turned into a pillar of salt.*

—GENESIS 19:23–26

In my imagination Lot's wife sometimes walks beside me with gentle, or not-so-gentle, reminders that if I look back and focus my attention on the regrets and failures of the past, I will become corrosive with resentment. She reminds me that I don't want to end up like she did.

Genesis 19:15–29
Psalm 26
Matthew 8:23–27

# JUNE 29

• ST. PETER AND ST. PAUL, APOSTLES •

*I sought the LORD, and he answered me*
*and delivered me from all my fears.*
*Look to him that you may be radiant with joy;*
*and your faces may not blush with shame.*
*When the poor one called out, the LORD heard,*
*and from all his distress he saved him.*

—PSALM 34:4–6

Peter and Paul might have turned to this psalm as they passed through trials and rescues. They might have recalled what they were before the Spirit of God tranformed them. Peter could reflect on his moment of denial and Paul on his track record of persecution. Their stories lend enormous hope; when we, in our poverty, turn toward the light of Christ, there will be no limit to what it calls forth in us.

| **Vigil** | **Day** |
|---|---|
| Acts 3:1–10 | Acts 12:1–11 |
| Psalm 19 | Psalm 34 |
| Galatians 1:11–20 | 2 Timothy 4:6–8, 17–18 |
| John 21:15–19 | Matthew 16:13–19 |

*Thursday*

# JUNE 30

• THE FIRST HOLY MARTYRS OF THE HOLY ROMAN CHURCH •

*Those who sow in tears*
*shall reap rejoicing.*
*Although they go forth weeping,*
*carrying the seed to be sown,*
*They shall come back rejoicing,*
*carrying their sheaves.*
—PSALM 126: 5–6

When the sorrows and tears bring us to a dark place, God is waiting there to hold us. When we sow heartbreak, only God can see what the final result will be: fruitfulness and joy.

Genesis 22:1–19
Psalm 126 (from Common of Martyrs)
Matthew 9:1–8

*Friday*

# JULY 1

• SACRED HEART OF JESUS •

*Come to me, all you who labor and are burdened, and I will give you rest. Take my yoke upon you and learn from me, for I am meek and humble of heart; and you will find rest for yourselves. For my yoke is easy, and my burden light.*

—MATTHEW 11:28–30

When I surrender to your yoke, I discover that it is a double yoke; you plow every field and furrow of my life right there alongside me, teaching, guiding, and giving balance and rest.

Deuteronomy 7:6–11
Psalm 103
1 John 4:7–16
Matthew 11:25–30

*And [Jesus] said to them, "Why were you looking for me? Did you not*
*know that I must be in my Father's house?"*
—LUKE 2:49

Pablo Picasso once said, "Tradition is about having a baby,
not wearing your grandfather's hat." Even as a youngster,
Jesus was finding his place in the traditions of Judaism, yet
beginning to find his own path of calling, to bring God to
us anew.

Genesis 27:1–5, 15–29
Psalm 135
Luke 2:41–51

*Sunday*

# JULY 3

*See, your king shall come to you;*
*a just savior is he,*
*Meek, and riding on an ass,*
*on a colt, the foal of an ass.*
*. . . [He] shall proclaim peace to the nations.*
—ZECHARIAH 9:9–10

This is a far cry from what we expect to see under the heading "Triumphant"—the very opposite of the victory parades that strut through human history. Here comes a victorious conqueror who arrives on a donkey, a conqueror who has overcome the ultimate enemy, death, and brings the spoils of victory—peace! Not a negotiated settlement, but unconditional, life-giving, all-embracing peace!

Zechariah 9:9–10
Psalm 145
Romans 8:9, 11–13
Matthew 11:25–30

*Monday*

# JULY 4

*When [Jacob] came upon a certain shrine, as the sun had already set,*
*he stopped there for the night. Taking one of the stones at the shrine, he*
*put it under his head and lay down to sleep at that spot. Then he had*
*a dream: a stairway rested on the ground, with its top reaching to the*
*heavens; and God's messengers were going up and down on it.*

—GENESIS 28:11–12

Sometimes the hardest, stoniest parts of our lives can
become the very places in which the ladders appear that
connect us to God.

Genesis 28:10–22
Psalm 91
Matthew 9:18–26

---

≥ 219 ≤

*Then some man wrestled with him until the break of dawn. When the man saw that he could not prevail over him, he struck Jacob's hip at its socket, so that the hip socket was wrenched as they wrestled. The man then said, "Let me go, for it is daybreak." But Jacob said, "I will not let you go until you bless me."*

—GENESIS 32:25–27

The problems we wrestle with can sometimes become the experiences that most bless us, if we are willing to learn from the struggles.

Genesis 32:23–33
Psalm 17
Matthew 9:32–38

*Thus, since there was a famine in the land of Canaan also, the sons of Israel were among those who came to procure rations.*
*It was Joseph, as governor of the country, who dispensed the rations to all the people. When Joseph's brothers came and knelt down before him with their faces to the ground, he recognized them as soon as he saw them. . . [He] locked them up in the guardhouse for three days.*

—GENESIS 42:5–7, 17

Joseph, once left for dead by his brothers, now keeps them in a different kind of tomb—three days in custody— before facilitating their resurrection. The time of darkness precedes and leads to the moment of recognition, remorse, and reconciliation.

Genesis 41:55–57, 42:5–7, 17–24
Psalm 33
Matthew 10:1–7

*"Come closer to me," he told his brothers. When they had done so, he said: "I am your brother Joseph, whom you once sold into Egypt. But now do not be distressed, and do not reproach yourselves for having sold me here. It was really for the sake of saving lives that God sent me here ahead of you."*

—GENESIS 45:4–5

It's been said that God writes straight with crooked lines. The story of Joseph and his brothers is a very crooked line indeed, involving a dysfunctional family, a web of deception, abduction into slavery, and a rise to political stardom. And it all leads to an outcome, in God's providence, that ensures the greater good for all concerned. Can we believe that this might be true for our own crooked lines?

Genesis 44:18–21, 23–29, 45:1–5
Psalm 105
Matthew 10:7–15

*Behold, I am sending you like sheep in the midst of wolves; so be shrewd as serpents and simple as doves.*

—MATTHEW 10:16

The Shepherd who counts us among his flock isn't expecting us to be mindless followers. God desires that we learn from him the art of combining a soft heart with a sharp mind.

Genesis 46:1–7, 28–30
Psalm 37
Matthew 10:16–23

*Nothing is concealed that will not be revealed, nor secret that will not be known. What I say to you in the darkness, speak in the light; what you hear whispered, proclaim on the housetops.*

—MATTHEW 10:26–27

When the masks are discarded and we dare to emerge
from behind our many protective disguises, then the real
you and the real me will be revealed. It's only a matter of
time and courage and, above all, grace.

Genesis 49:29–32, 50:15–26
Psalm 105
Matthew 10:24–33

*Sunday*

# JULY 10

*Just as from the heavens
the rain and snow come down
And do not return there
till they have watered the earth,
making it fertile and fruitful,
. . . So shall my word be
. . . My word shall not return to me void,
but shall do my will,
achieving the end for which I sent it.*

—ISAIAH 55:10–11

Who would imagine how many wildflower seeds were tossed by the autumn winds until the tiny blooms open as the warm air awakens them? We cannot know what God has planted within us—or what will call it forth.

Isaiah 55:10–11
Psalm 65
Romans 8:18–23
Matthew 13:1–23 or 13:1–9

*Then would the waters have overwhelmed us;*
*. . . Blessed be the LORD, who did not leave us*
*a prey to their teeth.*

—PSALM 124:4–6

In January of 2005 the crew of the geological survey
ship noticed a figure drifting on the waters off the coast
of Southeast Asia. Swept out to sea by the force of the
tsunami, a twelve-year-old Norwegian girl had clung to a
piece of driftwood for days, in deep shock. The sailors,
hardened men of the world, wept for joy as they made her
comfortable on board. The captain who, amazingly, was
also Norwegian, gently coaxed her back to life by speaking
to her in her native tongue.

Exodus 1:8–14, 22
Psalm 124
Matthew 10:34—1:1

*Pharaoh's daughter came down to the river to bathe, while her maids walked along the river bank. Noticing the basket among the reeds, she sent her handmaid to fetch it. On opening it, she looked, and lo, there was a baby boy, crying!*

—EXODUS 2:5–6

Every new life begins in mystery and is discovered where we least expect it. What discoveries await us among the reeds and rushes of our journey with God? Will we recognize them for what they are?

Exodus 2:1–15
Psalm 69
Matthew 11:20–24

*Remove the sandals from your feet, for the place where you stand
is holy ground.*

—EXODUS 3:5

We stand before a burning bush whenever other human
beings share with us something of their relationship with
God or something of the movements of their hearts.
In such moments may we always realize that we stand
on holy ground.

Exodus 3:1–6, 9–12
Psalm 103
Matthew 11:25–27

*Thursday*

# JULY 14

• BD. KATERI TEKAKWITHA, VIRGIN •

*Moses . . . said to [God], "When I go to the children of Israel and say to them, 'The God of your fathers has sent me to you,' if they ask me, 'What is his name?' what am I to tell them?" God replied, "I am who am."*

—EXODUS 3:13–14

We attach many names to the mystery we call God, and we project many flawed images onto that One. Yet we can't really capture God through anything we think, say, or express. We rely on what God reveals to us of God's self.

Exodus 3:13–20
Psalm 105
Matthew 11:28–30

*Friday*

# JULY 15

• ST. BONAVENTURE, BISHOP AND DOCTOR OF THE CHURCH •

*If you knew what this meant, "I desire mercy, not sacrifice," you would
not have condemned these innocent men.*

—MATTHEW 12:7

God is not asking us to appease God's wrath but to accept
God's loving-kindness.

Exodus 11:10 – 12:14
Psalm 116
Matthew 12:1–8

*He will not contend or cry out,*
*nor will anyone hear his voice in the streets.*
*A bruised reed he will not break,*
*a smoldering wick he will not quench,*
*until he brings justice to victory.*

—MATTHEW 12:19–20

When we have to raise our voices, we have already lost
the argument.

When we resort to violence, we have betrayed
our humanity.

When we extinguish another person's hope, something
in ourselves dies, too.

Exodus 12:37–42
Psalm 136
Matthew 12:14–21

*If you pull up the weeds you might uproot the wheat along with them.*
*Let them grow together until harvest.*

—MATTHEW 13:29–30

Our life's gardens are full of hybrids. We do good things
from selfish motives; we do harm when we are trying to
help. How reassuring to hear that we can safely leave it to
God to sort the good plants from the weeds.

Wisdom 12:13, 16–19
Psalm 86
Romans 8:26–27
Matthew 13:24–43 or 13:24–30

# JULY 18

*They complained to Moses, "Were there no burial places in Egypt that you had to bring us out here to die in the desert? Why did you do this to us? Why did you bring us out of Egypt? Did we not tell you this in Egypt, when we said, 'Leave us alone. Let us serve the Egyptians'? Far better for us to be the slaves of the Egyptians than to die in the desert."*

—EXODUS 14:11–12

Within weeks of the collapse of the Berlin Wall there were voices in the former East Germany expressing a wish to have it back again. Sometimes it is just too demanding to live with freedom and the personal responsibility that comes along with it.

Exodus 14:5–18
Exodus 15:1–6
Matthew 12:38–42

*[Jesus said], "Who is my mother? Who are my brothers?" And stretching out his hand toward his disciples, he said, "Here are my mother and my brothers. For whoever does the will of my heavenly Father is my brother, and sister, and mother."*

—MATTHEW 12:48–50

What an extended family we have! When they look at us, will they see brothers and sisters, too?

Exodus 14:21—15:1
Exodus 15:8–10, 12, 17
Matthew 12:46–50

*Then the LORD said to Moses, "I will now rain down bread from heaven for you. Each day the people are to go out and gather their daily portion."*

—EXODUS 16:4

We pray for "our daily bread," but actually we want at least a week's supply—just in case! Manna comes only in one-day portions. If we try to hoard it, it will spoil. Manna is one of God's many ways of saying, "Live in the present moment and trust me for the rest."

Exodus 16:1–5, 9–15
Psalm 78
Matthew 13:1–9

*Blessed are your eyes, because they see, and your ears, because they hear. Amen, I say to you, many prophets and righteous people longed to see what you see but did not see it, and to hear what you hear but did not hear it.*

—MATTHEW 13:16–17

Not all the books in the world's libraries or all the learning of the world's teachers and philosophers amount to even a moment of awareness when God's power and love touch our personal experience.

Exodus 19:1–2, 9–11, 16–20
Daniel 3:52–56
Matthew 13:10–17

*The watchmen came upon me,*
*as they made their rounds of the city:*
*Have you seen him whom my heart loves?*
*I had hardly left them*
*when I found him whom my heart loves.*
—SONG OF SONGS 3:3–4

Mary Magdalene's story is one we can identify with readily—of longing, loving, and losing, of searching and rediscovering the beloved in the most unexpected circumstances. But as we celebrate her feast day, we are invited to follow Mary's search to the garden of the Resurrection. We are encouraged to travel with her as Jesus sends her out, the first apostle of the risen Christ.

Song of Songs 3:1–4 or 2 Corinthians 5:14–17
Psalm 63
John 20:1–2, 11–18

*God the LORD has spoken and summoned the earth,*
*from the rising of the sun to its setting.*
*From Zion, perfect in beauty,*
*God shines forth.*

—PSALM 50:1–2

After a seemingly endless night flight, the aircraft cruised
into the dawn. Below us, Africa was just waking. A band
of dawn-gold encircled the earth, like a ring of covenant,
a beautiful reminder that God's love encircles our lives
from dawn to dusk to dawn, wherever in the world we may
find ourselves.

Exodus 24:3–8
Psalm 50
Matthew 13:24–30

*The kingdom of heaven is like a treasure buried in a field, which a person finds and hides again, and out of joy goes and sells all that he has and buys that field.*

—MATTHEW 13:44

A television commercial tells us that while we can buy much of what we desire with a particular credit card, some things will always remain priceless. When we find the priceless treasure, we will let go of everything else, just to hold that treasure.

1 Kings 3:5, 7–12
Psalm 119
Romans 8:28–30
Matthew 13:44–52 or 13:44–46

*Whoever wishes to be great among you shall be your servant; whoever wishes to be first among you shall be your slave. Just so, the Son of Man did not come to be served but to serve and to give his life as a ransom for many.*

—MATTHEW 20:26–28

Today we celebrate the feast of an apostle whose mother once argued for his right to sit next to Jesus in the kingdom, and we listen to Jesus' response to this request. We still haven't got the message, either in our public or church life or in our personal life. Yet today's readings give us hope that the kingdom will indeed reverse all our expectations, and when it does, we shall recognize and welcome it.

2 Corinthians 4:7–15
Psalm 126
Matthew 20:20–28

*Tuesday*

# JULY 26

• ST. JOACHIM AND ST. ANN, PARENTS OF THE BLESSED VIRGIN MARY •

*Now will I praise those godly men,*
*our ancestors, each in his own time.*

—SIRACH 44:1

Today should be Grandparents' Day! Joachim and Ann,
traditionally named as the parents of Mary, would surely
have seen Jesus through grandparents' eyes. Grandparents
are often the ones who see and hear the things little children
say and do, and realize their significance. They have the
eyes to see and the ears to hear what the busy parents
might easily miss. We can all take a little extra time and
care to listen and attend to a child, whether or not we have
our own. When we do this, we might experience the joy
promised by Jesus and surely known by Joachim and Ann.

Exodus 33:7–11; 34:5–9, 28
Sirach 44:1, 10–15 (from Memorial)
Psalm 103
Matthew 13:36–43

*The Kingdom of heaven is like a merchant searching for fine pearls. When he finds a pearl of great price, he goes and sells all that he has and buys it.*

—MATTHEW 13:45–46

Jake's parents used all their savings and sold their home to pay for life-saving surgery for their only child. God gives everything for each of us, as if each one were God's only child, valued beyond all price.

Exodus 34:29–35
Psalm 99
Matthew 13:44–46

*Every scribe who has been instructed in the Kingdom of heaven is like the head of a household who brings from his storeroom both the new and the old.*

—MATTHEW 13:52

To follow Jesus is to value the traditions of yesterday and build on them to create tomorrow.

Exodus 40:16–21, 34–38
Psalm 84
Matthew 13:47–53

*Friday*

# JULY 29

• ST. MARTHA •

*There shall be no strange god among you*
*nor shall you worship an alien god.*
*I, the LORD, am your God*
*who led you forth from the land of Egypt.*

—PSALM 16:3–4

If we think this warning is not about us, let us take a stroll
through the shopping mall, browse the celebrity gossip
magazines, watch a typical Hollywood movie, and meet
some of our own century's alien gods face to face.

Leviticus 23:1, 4–11, 15–16, 27, 34–37
Psalm 81
John 11:19–27 or Luke 10:38–42

*At a birthday celebration for Herod, the daughter of Herodias performed a dance before the guests and delighted Herod so much that he swore to give her whatever she might ask for. Prompted by her mother, she said, "Give me here on a platter the head of John the Baptist." The king was distressed, but because of his oaths and the guests who were present, he ordered that it be given, and he had John beheaded in the prison.*

—MATTHEW 14:6–10

The things we do to save face can cost us our immortal souls.

Leviticus 25:1, 8–17
Psalm 67
Matthew 14:1–12

*All you who are thirsty,*
*come to the water!*
*You who have no money,*
*come, receive grain and eat;*
*Come without paying and without cost,*
*drink wine and milk!*

—ISAIAH 55:1

Severe weather cut off the little town, closing the roads, causing power failures, and leaving the townspeople without warmth or food. But they discovered something more important than home comforts; they turned to one another not to ask for help but to offer it. Very soon an average town had turned into a living community.

Isaiah 55:1–3
Psalm 145
Romans 8:35, 37–39
Matthew 14:13–21

*Peter got out of the boat and began to walk on the water toward Jesus.*
*But when he saw how strong the wind was he became frightened; and,*
*beginning to sink, he cried out, "Lord, save me!" Immediately Jesus*
*stretched out his hand and caught him.*

—MATTHEW 14:29–31

We tend to see only that Peter lost faith and began to sink.
What we forget is that he really did walk on water with
Jesus! Sometimes we continue with Jesus only by trying
and failing, losing our faith, and then finding it again.

Numbers 11:4–15
Psalm 81
Matthew 14:22–36

# AUGUST 2

*After [sending the crowds away], he went up on the mountain by himself to pray. When it was evening he was there alone. Meanwhile the boat, already a few miles offshore, was being tossed about by the waves, for the wind was against it.*

—MATTHEW 14:23–24

Jesus is at prayer. His disciples are at sea. In the calm of his communion with God, he is most deeply and powerfully present to his friends' battle with the elements. His prayer is what they need, above all, in their struggle. In prayer Jesus is drawing on the saving power of God for all of them.

Numbers 12:1–13
Psalm 51
Matthew 14:22–36 or Matthew 15:1–2, 10–14

*He said in reply, "It is not right to take the food of the children and throw it to the dogs." She said, "Please, Lord, for even the dogs eat the scraps that fall from the table of their masters."*

—MATTHEW 15:26–27

It takes a pretty strong kind of faith to challenge Jesus, to dare to ask our questions, to make our point, or to plead our case when what we are feeling runs counter to orthodoxy. How do we feel about expressing our real feelings in our prayer? God welcomes us just as we are and responds to who we really are, underneath our veneer of political correctness.

Numbers 13:1–2, 25—14:1, 26–29, 34–35
Psalm 106
Matthew 15:21–28

*Thursday*

# AUGUST 4

*The LORD said to Moses, "Take your staff and assemble the community, you and your brother Aaron, and in their presence order the rock to yield its waters. From the rock you shall bring forth water for the congregation and their livestock to drink."*

—NUMBERS 20:7–8

The freshest water often flows out of the hardest rock. The hard places of our lives often yield the greatest wisdom, for ourselves and for the whole community.

Numbers 20:1–13
Psalm 95
Matthew 16:13–23

# AUGUST 5

*Jesus said to his disciples, "Whoever wishes to come after me must deny himself, take up his cross, and follow me. For whoever wishes to save his life will lose it, but whoever loses his life for my sake will find it."*

—MATTHEW 16:24–25

To follow Jesus is to be willing to walk with trust even through the worst apparent disasters and in doing so to discover that on the other side of breakdown is a breakthrough to a dimension of being far beyond anything we can ask or imagine. This is the heart of our believing. This is the Good News of Calvary.

Deuteronomy 4:32–40
Psalm 77
Matthew 16:24–28

*Moreover, we possess the prophetic message that is altogether reliable.*
*You will do well to be attentive to it, as to a lamp shining in a dark*
*place, until day dawns and the morning star rises in your hearts.*

—2 PETER 1:19

A thin, wavering beam of spiritual understanding and
prophetic insight lights a stumbling way through history,
guiding those who are willing to follow in trust until the
all-transfiguring light shall shine upon all creation and
banish our doubt and confusion.

Daniel 7:9–10, 13–14
Psalm 97
2 Peter 1:16–19
Matthew 17:1–9

# AUGUST 7

*He said, "Come." Peter got out of the boat and began to walk on the
water toward Jesus. But when he saw how strong the wind was he
became frightened; and, beginning to sink, he cried out, "Lord, save me!"*

—MATTHEW 14:29–30

More than once I, too, have embarked on some new
venture that was going to push me beyond my comfort
zone. And more than once I have been fine until I met the
winds of opposition and my resolve began to sink. Trust
can be a very slow-growing plant.

1 Kings 19:9, 11–13
Psalm 85
Romans 9:1–5
Matthew 14:22–33

# AUGUST 8

• ST. DOMINIC, PRIEST •

*So you too must befriend the alien, for you were once aliens yourselves in the land of Egypt.*

—DEUTERONOMY 10:19

Our most human, most Christ-like qualities are often forged in the times of hardship. Suffering can be the mother of true empathy. Let us therefore not desperately try to avoid it, but rather let it become our teacher.

Deuteronomy 10:12–22
Psalm 147
Matthew 17:22–27

⇒ 254 ⇐

# AUGUST 9

*Be brave and steadfast; have no fear or dread of them, for it is the LORD, your God, who marches with you; he will never fail you or forsake you.*

—DEUTERONOMY 31:6

George is a thoroughgoing bad-news merchant. Nothing seems to please him more than being the first to phone around his acquaintances to tell them about some accident, sickness, or other misfortune that has struck someone's life. George isn't alone in his perversity. The world is full of people who enjoy disheartening others. The Lord is the antidote to every George on earth. The Lord leads us fearlessly past the disheartening information and toward the fullness of his love.

Deuteronomy 31:1–8
Deuteronomy 32:3–4, 7–9, 12
Matthew 18:1–5, 10, 12–14

*The one who supplies seed to the sower and bread for food will supply and multiply your seed and increase the harvest of your righteousness.*

—2 CORINTHIANS 9:10

When I think of St. Lawrence, I travel mentally to eastern Canada and the St. Lawrence Seaway, named for him by the first European settlers. I think he would also have appreciated the connection; he was a deacon commissioned to provide for others. The first settlers arrived, often penniless, at the great estuary of the St. Lawrence and then spread out all over the continent to sow their meager seeds and work for a difficult living or, sometimes, a hard death. This is a model of the deacon's work and a model for each of us, to sow the seeds of love and generosity to the best of our ability.

2 Corinthians 9:6–10
Psalm 112
John 12:24–26

# AUGUST 11

• ST. CLARE, VIRGIN •

*His master summoned him and said to him, "You wicked servant! I forgave you your entire debt because you begged me to. Should you not have had pity on your fellow servant, as I had pity on you?"*

—MATTHEW 18:32–33

Derek begged his employer to give him another chance after he had lost an important contract through a series of errors and miscalculations. When his appeal was granted, he almost danced home in relief. But that night he lashed out at his little son for not doing his homework properly.

Joshua 3:7–11, 13–17
Psalm 114
Matthew 18:21—19:1

*I gave you a land that you had not tilled and cities that you had not built, to dwell in; you have eaten of vineyards and olive groves which you did not plant.*

—JOSHUA 24:13

Every aspect of my life—my home, my clothes, my food—comes to me through the labor and the love of many others. I am utterly dependent on the web of relatedness that holds everything together. The only possible response to such gifting is an attitude of permanent thanksgiving.

Joshua 24:1–13
Psalm 136
Matthew 19:3–12

# AUGUST 13

*Then the people promised Joshua, "We will serve the LORD, our God, and obey his voice."*

—JOSHUA 24:24

They say it, and they mean it. We say it, too, and we think we mean it, but will we live as though we meant it? Will our actions bear out our acclamations? Let us listen carefully today to hear the voice we have promised to obey.

Joshua 24:14–29
Psalm 16
Matthew 19:13–15

*The foreigners who join themselves to the LORD,*
*ministering to him,*
*Loving the name of the LORD,*
*and becoming his servants—*
*All who keep the sabbath free from profanation*
*and hold to my covenant,*
*Them I will bring to my holy mountain*
*and make joyful in my house of prayer.*

—ISAIAH 56:6

The holy mountain has wide and welcoming slopes. God
has not given us leave to exclude anyone, for any reason,
from God's all-embracing love or from God's open house
and table of fellowship.

Isaiah 56:1, 6–7
Psalm 67
Romans 11:13–15, 29–32
Matthew 15:21–28

*Monday*

# AUGUST 15

• ASSUMPTION OF THE BLESSED VIRGIN MARY •

*He has cast down the mighty from their thrones,*
*and has lifted up the lowly.*
*He has filled the hungry with good things,*
*and the rich he has sent away empty.*

—LUKE 1:52–53

As we celebrate the raising of a poor, humble girl from the Middle East to heaven's heights, we remember her great song of praise. In God's kingdom, everything we've established is upturned, just as a farmer plows a field, and people walking familiar paths through the grass suddenly discover those paths churned up. When Jesus walks the fields of Galilee, our path is radically disturbed, but for those who have been marginalized and despised, there is a bountiful feast.

| Vigil | Mass |
|-------|------|
| 1 Chronicles 15:3–4, 15–16; 16:1–2 | Revelation 11:19; 12:1–6, 10 |
| Psalm 132 | Psalm 45 |
| 1 Corinthians 15:54–57 | 1 Corinthians 15:20–27 |
| Luke 11:27–28 | Luke 1:39–56 |

# AUGUST 16

*But many who are first will be last, and the last will be first.*
—MATTHEW 19:30

Joe was never going to be at the top of the class. He had learning difficulties, and he wasn't very steady on his feet. He wasn't going to win any races. Sometimes other children made fun of him. Sometimes even the teachers became impatient. But when the flu epidemic struck the school, it was little, slow Joe who was right there, looking after the younger ones, tidying up the classrooms, and keeping everyone's spirits up with his gentle smile.

Judges 6:11–24
Psalm 85
Matthew 19:23–30

# AUGUST 17

*Take what is yours and go. What if I wish to give this last one the same as you? Or am I not free to do as I wish with my own money? Are you envious because I am generous?*

—MATTHEW 20:14–15

Fairness is a human virtue.

God's generosity is something else.

Judges 9:6–15
Psalm 21
Matthew 20:1–16

# AUGUST 18

*Then the king said to his servants, "The feast is ready, but those who were invited were not worthy to come. Go out, therefore, into the main roads and invite to the feast whomever you find."*

—MATTHEW 22:8–9

I wonder where the host will find us? Among those who were sent official invitations to the kingdom but never showed up? Or will he gather us in from the crossroads?

Judges 11:29–39
Psalm 40
Matthew 22:1–14

*But Ruth said, "Do not ask me to abandon or forsake you! for wherever you go I will go, wherever you lodge I will lodge, your people shall be my people, and your God my God."*

—RUTH 1:16

It's a promise that we might make to another person if we really loved that person with all our heart.

It's a promise that God makes to every one of us personally. What does that say about how much God loves us!

Ruth 1:1, 3–6, 14–16, 22
Psalm 146
Matthew 22:34–40

*The greatest among you must be your servant. Whoever exalts himself will be humbled; but whoever humbles himself will be exalted.*

—MATTHEW 23:11–12

When we presume to occupy the moral high ground and imagine ourselves to be above reproach or correction, then we will miss the One who walks among the humble, the needy, and the lost.

Ruth 2:1–3, 8–11; 4:13–17
Psalm 128
Matthew 23:1–12

*"For who has known the mind of the Lord
or who has been his counselor?
Or who has given him anything
that he may be repaid?"
For from him and through him and for him are all things. To him be
glory forever. Amen.*

—ROMANS 11:34–36

I wonder how many of our prayers amount to us advising God about how to run our world. Do we seek God's guidance, or just God's approval of and help with what we have already decided for ourselves?

Perhaps every time of prayer should begin and end with a reflection on these words from Paul.

Isaiah 22:19–23
Psalm 138
Romans 11:33–36
Matthew 16:13–20

*Woe to you, scribes and Pharisees, you hypocrites. You lock the Kingdom of heaven before men. You do not enter yourselves, nor do you allow entrance to those trying to enter.*

—MATTHEW 23:13

Once upon a time there was a beautiful garden owned by a jealous landowner. He built a high wall around it to keep out the people he disapproved of. And then—imagine!— he had to spend all his waking moments patrolling the boundary wall to make sure no one unacceptable got in. In all his efforts, he died, never having enjoyed his own garden.

God forbid that such a scenario arise—especially among God's people.

1 Thessalonians 1:1–5, 8–10
Psalm 149
Matthew 23:13–22

*Blind Pharisee, cleanse first the inside of the cup, so that the outside also may be clean.*

—MATTHEW 23:26

The things that defile us begin in our hearts and spread to our hands and feet and lips, and finally to the rest of the world and all creation.

Jesus invites us to let God cleanse our hearts and break the cycle of pollution.

1 Thessalonians 2:1–8
Psalm 139
Matthew 23:23–26

# AUGUST 24

• ST. BARTHOLOMEW, APOSTLE •

*Philip found Nathanael and told him, "We have found the one about whom Moses wrote in the law, and also the prophets, Jesus, son of Joseph, from Nazareth." But Nathanael said to him, "Can anything good come from Nazareth?" Philip said to him, "Come and see."*

—JOHN 1:45–46

St. Bartholomew is traditionally believed to have been Nathanael, who here reveals his cynicism that "anything good could come out of Nazareth." I know a lovely retreat house on the western coast of Australia, called Nathanael's Rest. It is named for Nathanael because it is a place where people who have perhaps become hardened by disappointment and cynicism can drink from a deeper well and accept the open-ended invitation to "come and see" just what this man from Nazareth is about.

Revelation 21:9–14
Psalm 145
John 1:45–51

*A thousand years in your sight*
*are as yesterday, now that it is past,*
*or as a watch of the night.*

—PSALM 90:4

And so the miracle that turns a grain of wheat into a loaf of bread over many months, or a human person into a reflection of God over many years, is no less wondrous than the instantaneous miracles of Scripture.

1 Thessalonians 3:7–13
Psalm 90
Matthew 24:42–51

# AUGUST 26

*The mountains melt like wax before the LORD,*
*before the LORD of all the earth.*

—PSALM 97:5

I watched the sun set over the Alps, leaving the famous alpenglow behind, to fade into dusk. Then, as darkness covered the earth, a million stars took the place of our one star and set the night alight. How could my heart not overflow with joy in the presence of such glory?

1 Thessalonians 4:1–8
Psalm 97
Matthew 25:1–13

*For to everyone who has, more will be given and he will grow rich; but from the one who has not, even what he has will be taken away.*

—MATTHEW 25:29

Gifts are given to be spent. The more we spend them, the more they regenerate themselves. But if we hold on to them, for our own good alone, they shrivel away for lack of use.

1 Thessalonians 4:9–11
Psalm 98
Matthew 25:14–30

# AUGUST 28

*Get behind me, Satan! You are an obstacle to me. You are thinking not as God does, but as human beings do.*

—MATTHEW 16:23

Even things that seem very good can become obstacles to our onward journey. Here Jesus rebukes one of his closest, chosen friends, whose failure to understand is proving a roadblock. We may not even recognize the things that are blocking us, for our thoughts are not God's thoughts, and our eyes do not see as God sees.

Jeremiah 20:7–9
Psalm 63
Romans 12:1–2
Matthew 16:21–27

*Herodias's own daughter came in and performed a dance that delighted Herod and his guests. The king said to the girl, "Ask of me whatever you wish and I will grant it to you."... She said, "I want you to give me at once on a platter the head of John the Baptist." The king was deeply distressed, but because of his oaths and the guests he did not wish to break his word to her. So he promptly dispatched an executioner with orders to bring back his head. He went off and beheaded him in the prison.*

—MARK 6:22–23, 25–26

An innocent man loses his life so that a guilty man can save his honor. This ancient atrocity is repeated year after year as we defend our national and personal pride, no matter the cost in innocent lives or to the poor and helpless. May we be as critical of our own strategies as we are of Herod.

1 Thessalonians 4:13–18
Psalm 96
Mark 6:17–29

*I believe I shall see the bounty of the LORD*
*in the land of the living.*
*Wait for the LORD with courage;*
*be stouthearted, and wait for the LORD.*

—PSALM 27:13–14

Monuments and cathedrals are fine, but God's goodness becomes visible in human lives and living people. Our hope lies in what God can do in us.

1 Thessalonians 5:1–6, 9–11
Psalm 27
Luke 4:31–37

*I, like a green olive tree*
*in the house of God,*
*Trust the mercy of God*
*forever and ever.*
—PSALM 52:10

A tree in the midst of a house—a living, growing reality in the heart of whatever structures and institutions we may build around it. That is a promise we can trust, a reason for hope.

Colossians 1:1–8
Psalm 52
Luke 4:38–44

*After [Jesus] had finished speaking, he said to Simon, "Put out into deep water and lower your nets for a catch."*

—LUKE 5:4

The greatest danger to shipping is not the sea but the land. Many shipwrecks happen because ships try to stay in water that's too shallow and run aground on the rocks and sandbanks.

Jesus warns us not to make the same mistake in our spiritual journey.

Colossians 1:9–14
Psalm 98
Luke 5:1–11

# SEPTEMBER 2

*He is before all things,*
*and in him all things hold together.*
—COLOSSIANS 1:17

Our spirits are at home in the One who is both beyond
and within space-time, the One who is infinite mystery and
deepest intimacy, the One who holds us in being and frees
us to become who we are. We are because God *is*.

Colossians 1:15–20
Psalm 100
Luke 5:33–39

*While Jesus was going through a field of grain on a sabbath, his disciples were picking the heads of grain, rubbing them in their hands, and eating them. Some Pharisees said, "Why are you doing what is unlawful on the sabbath?" Jesus said to them in reply, "Have you not read what David did when he and those who were with him were hungry? How he went into the house of God, took the bread of offering, which only the priests could lawfully eat, ate of it, and shared it with his companions?" Then he said to them, "The Son of Man is lord of the sabbath."*

—LUKE 6:1–5

We are more important than our rules, and the people on whom we impose our rules are more important than our rules. Also, the One who gives us the ability to make the rules offers us the freedom to rise above them.

Colossians 1:21–23
Psalm 54
Luke 6:1–5

*Sunday*

# SEPTEMBER 4

*Owe nothing to anyone, except to love one another; for the one who loves another has fulfilled the law. The commandments, "You shall not commit adultery; you shall not kill; you shall not steal; you shall not covet," and whatever other commandment there may be, are summed up in this saying, namely, "You shall love your neighbor as yourself."*
—ROMANS 13:8–10

Not only our bank balance but also our energy balance can go into deficit. We slip into negative energy whenever we feed the fears, resentments, and discontent around us and within us. Eventually this movement will bankrupt us spiritually.

Ezekiel 33:7–9
Psalm 95
Romans 13:8–10
Matthew 18:15–20

*Looking around at them all, [Jesus] then said to him, "Stretch out your hand." He did so and his hand was restored.*

—LUKE 6:10

In her grief and loss, Grace turned in on herself. Her sorrow ran its course. Her healing began when she reached the point where she could stretch out her hand again to support others.

Colossians 1:24—2:3
Psalm 62
Luke 6:6–11

# SEPTEMBER 6

*Jesus departed to the mountain to pray, and he spent the night in prayer to God. When day came, he called his disciples to himself, and from them he chose Twelve, whom he also named Apostles.*

—LUKE 6:12–13

Jesus understood that wise decisions and wise actions must be rooted in contemplation. Whom he chose to be apostles would have an impact throughout history; those hours of prayer would bear much fruit.

Colossians 2:6–15
Psalm 145
Luke 6:12–19

*For you have died, and your life is hidden with Christ in God. When
Christ your life appears, then you too will appear with him in glory.*

—COLOSSIANS 3:3–4

When I hold an acorn in my hand, I can only try to
imagine the mighty forest it has the potential to become.
The seeds of who we can become lie in God's hand, who
alone knows the shape of their fulfillment.

Colossians 3:1–11
Psalm 145
Luke 6:20–26

*I trust in your faithfulness. Grant my heart joy in your help,*
*That I may sing of the LORD, "How good our God has been to me!"*

—PSALM 13:6

There's no human act so radical as giving birth to new life.
We don't know what that life will demand of us or what
difficulties that daughter or son will face. In the case of the
birth we celebrate today, that act of trust results in the life
of the girl who in turn will give birth to New Life for the
whole of humanity. In bringing up this child, she will have
to trust God every moment of every day.

Micah 5:1–4 or Romans 8:28–30
Psalm 13
Matthew 1:1–16, 18–23 or 1:18–23

*Why do you notice the splinter in your brother's eye, but do not
perceive the wooden beam in your own?*

—LUKE 6:41

We shoot off our judgments and criticisms like arrows, but
they come hurtling back to us like boomerangs.

1 Timothy 1:1–2, 12–14
Psalm 16
Luke 6:39–42

*A good tree does not bear rotten fruit, nor does a rotten tree bear good fruit. For every tree is known by its own fruit. For people do not pick figs from thornbushes, nor do they gather grapes from brambles.*

—LUKE 6:43–44

If you want to measure our faith, do not ask what we believe, but rather ask what fruits our lives are offering to the world.

1 Timothy 1:15–17
Psalm 113
Luke 6:43–49

# SEPTEMBER 11

*Wrath and anger are hateful things,*
*yet the sinner hugs them tight.*
*The vengeful will suffer the LORD's vengeance,*
*for he remembers their sins in detail.*
*Forgive your neighbor's injustice;*
*then when you pray, your own sins will be forgiven.*

—SIRACH 27:30—28:2

Even the smallest mind and the meanest spirit is capable
of revenge. It takes a big person—a generous expanding
heart—to forgive.

Sirach 27:30—28:9
Psalm 103
Romans 14:7–9
Matthew 18:21–35

*It is my wish, then, that in every place the men should pray, lifting up
holy hands, without anger or argument.*

—1 TIMOTHY 2:8

Prayer—without anger directed against those who pray
differently.

A spiritual quest—without argument about which path is
the right path.

In every place such prayer should happen, not just in
church. And not only the men should pray!

1 Timothy 2:1–8
Psalm 28
Luke 7:1–10

*As he drew near to the gate of the city, a man who had died was being carried out, the only son of his mother, and she was a widow. A large crowd from the city was with her. When the Lord saw her, he was moved with pity for her and said to her, "Do not weep." He stepped forward and touched the coffin; at this the bearers halted, and he said, "Young man, I tell you, arise!" The dead man sat up and began to speak, and Jesus gave him to his mother.*

—LUKE 7:12–15

Jesus encounters death and touches it with compassion, sorrow, and then the gift of renewed life. Can we allow him to touch the dead parts of ourselves and trust him for the Resurrection?

1 Timothy 3:1–13
Psalm 101
Luke 7:11–17

*No one has gone up to heaven except the one who has come down from heaven, the Son of Man.*

—JOHN 3:13

The way of the cross is a two-way highway. The only way that the divine can reach the human is by way of the cross. The only way the human can reach up to the divine is by way of the cross. The cross is the crossroads at every journey to freedom and joy.

Numbers 21:4–9
Psalm 78
Philippians 2:6–11
John 3:13–17

*When Jesus saw his mother and the disciple there whom he loved, he said to his mother, "Woman, behold, your son." Then he said to the disciple, "Behold, your mother." And from that hour the disciple took her into his home.*

—JOHN 19:26–27

The only place where deep sorrow can be held safely is in loving relationship. Jesus knows this. And at the extremity of his anguish and the anguish of his mother and his friend, he seals this unique bond between them, which will hold them firm through all that is to come.

1 Timothy 4:12–16
Psalm 111
John 19:25–27 or Luke 2:33–35

⇒ 292 ⇐

*For we brought nothing into the world, just as we shall not be able to take anything out of it. If we have food and clothing, we shall be content with that.*

—1 TIMOTHY 6:7–8

When we are present at a birth or a death, we are reminded in a dramatic way that everything that occurs between those two moments is pure gift.

1 Timothy 6:2–12
Psalm 49
Luke 8:1–3

# SEPTEMBER 17

*Know that the LORD is God;*
*he made us, his we are;*
*his people, the flock he tends.*

—PSALM 100:3

God is the mystery who turns longing into be-longing.

1 Timothy 6:13–16
Psalm 100
Luke 8:4–15

*As high as the heavens are above the earth,*
*so high are my ways above your ways*
*and my thoughts above your thoughts.*

—ISAIAH 55:9

As the aircraft takes off, I can still recognize the familiar landmarks of my homeland. We rise, and the picture becomes hazy. We break through the cloud cover into a different dimension altogether. What we have left behind is miniscule compared to the vast expanse of the heavens. This shift in view gives us an idea of our own perceptions and understanding and of the awesome scale of what lies beyond us.

Isaiah 55:6–9
Psalm 145
Philippians 1:20–24, 27
Matthew 20:1–16

# SEPTEMBER 19

*No one who lights a lamp conceals it with a vessel or sets it under a bed; rather, he places it on a lampstand so that those who enter may see the light.*

—LUKE 8:16

Self-deprecation says, "My gifts are nothing." Genuine humility says, "Whatever gifts I may have are from God, and are for spending. What I can give may be small, but the world needs it."

Ezra 1:1–6
Psalm 126
Luke 8:16–18

# SEPTEMBER 20

• ST. ANDREW KIM TAEGON, PRIEST AND MARTYR, ST. PAUL CHONG
HASANG, MARTYR, AND THEIR COMPANIONS, MARTYRS •

*Jerusalem, built as a city*
*with compact unity.*
*To it the tribes go up,*
*the tribes of the LORD.*
—PSALM 122:3–4

Abraham has three sons. They were all born of the same
spirit. As they grew to adolescence they indulged in sibling
rivalry, fighting over the ancestral home and coming close
to destroying one another. One day, when they all grow
up, they will understand that what unites them is much
greater than what divides them.

Ezra 6:7–8, 12, 14–20
Psalm 122
Luke 8:19–21

# SEPTEMBER 21

*I . . . urge you to live in a manner worthy of the call you have received,*
*with all humility and gentleness, with patience, bearing with one*
*another through love, striving to preserve the unity of the spirit through*
*the bond of peace.*

—EPHESIANS 4:1–3

Not only the apostles and first disciples but we as well have
been called to this lovely and spirit-filled life. May our lives
be marked by unity and peace.

Ephesians 4:1–7, 11–13
Psalm 19
Matthew 9:9–13

*Is it time for you to dwell in your own paneled houses, while this house lies in ruins?*

—HAGGAI 1:4

This Scripture refers to the house of God. But we mustn't think of this as merely a structure, such as a cathedral or temple. The house of God was the home of the *community* known as God's people. How often, still, do we sacrifice community life for our individual, selfish interests?

Haggai 1:1–8
Psalm 149
Luke 9:7–9

*One moment yet, a little while,*
*and I will shake the heavens and the earth,*
*the sea and the dry land.*
*I will shake all the nations,*
*and the treasures of all the nations will come in,*
*and I will fill this house with glory,*
*says the LORD of hosts.*
*Mine is the silver and mine the gold,*
*says the LORD of hosts.*
—HAGGAI 2:6–8

Sometimes life has to shake us out of our complacency
and shatter our illusions and securities to set free the real
treasure in our lives.

Haggai 2:1–9
Psalm 43
Luke 9:18–22

*I will turn their mourning into joy,*
*I will console and gladden them after their sorrows.*

—JEREMIAH 31:13

After the devastating experience of losing her job and losing her home, Alice discovered a whole new dimension of herself as she turned her energies to caring for the homeless people in her neighborhood. She discovered for herself the truth of the prophetic word that great joy can come from what appears to be great sorrow.

Zechariah 2:5–9, 14–15
Jeremiah 31:10–13
Luke 9:43–45

*Amen, I say to you, tax collectors and prostitutes are entering the kingdom of God before you.*

—MATTHEW 21:31

Why are we so surprised that we see the ways of Jesus being lived out in practice in our twenty-first-century world by people of whom the church might well disapprove?

Ezekiel 18:25–28
Psalm 25
Philippians 2:1–11 or 2:1–5
Matthew 21:28–32

*Then John said in reply, "Master, we saw someone casting out demons in your name and we tried to prevent him because he does not follow in our company." Jesus said to him, "Do not prevent him, for whoever is not against you is for you."*

—LUKE 9:49–50

God's work transcends the boundaries of beliefs, groups, and labels. We should ask ourselves from time to time, "Where do I see God at work, outside of my own group?"

Zechariah 8:1–8
Psalm 102
Luke 9:46–50

*And he sent messengers ahead of him. On the way they entered a
Samaritan village to prepare for his reception there, but they would
not welcome him because the destination of his journey was Jerusalem.
When the disciples James and John saw this they asked, "Lord, do you
want us to call down fire from heaven to consume them?" Jesus turned
and rebuked them, and they journeyed to another village.*

—LUKE 9:52–56

Shall we unleash our superior military force on those we
deem our enemies? Shall we launch a preemptive strike?
Tell us, Lord!

He turned and rebuked them.

Zechariah 8:20–23
Psalm 87
Luke 9:51–56

*[To him Jesus said,] "No one who sets a hand to the plow and looks to what was left behind is fit for the Kingdom of God."*

—LUKE 9:62

As a river flows towards the ocean and never turns back, so our journeys with God can know only one direction: forward.

Nehemiah 2:1–8
Psalm 137
Luke 9:57–62

*"I say to you, you will see the sky opened and the angels of God
ascending and descending on the Son of Man."*

—JOHN 1:51

People say that angels come in many guises: the
unexpected moment of clear guidance, the protective
intervention, the person who touches your heart with
loving-wisdom and then disappears into the crowd. One
day we will see them everywhere; for now, let our hearts
be open, so that we don't miss them when they come upon
us unawares.

Daniel 7:9–10, 13–14 or Revelation 12:7–12
Psalm 138
John 1:47–51

*For we did not heed the voice of the Lord, our God, in all the words of the prophets whom he sent us, but each one of us went off after the devices of his own wicked heart, served other gods, and did evil in the sight of the Lord, our God.*

—BARUCH 1:21–22

What would the Old Testament prophets have to say if they walked the corridors of power today or lingered a while in our communities—even our church communities? Have we listened to them? Where might we hear the truth of their message today, and how might we respond?

Baruch 1:15–22
Psalm 79
Luke 10:13–16

# OCTOBER 1

*I have seen the captivity that the Eternal God has brought upon my sons and daughters. With joy I fostered them; but with mourning and lament I let them go.*

—BARUCH 4:10–11

We have seen our children taken captive, too, by a culture of drugs, sex, and street violence. We have also seen them taken captive by the financial institutions that deal in easy credit and have lured them into dependency on that most addictive substance: money. Drug pushing, money pushing—is there really any difference?

Baruch 4:5–12, 27–29
Psalm 69
Luke 10:17–24

*Once again, O LORD of hosts,*
*look down from heaven, and see;*
*Take care of this vine,*
*and protect what your right hand has planted.*
—PSALM 80:15–16

Every child born into this world is a precious seedling destined to become a vine of hope and transformation. We are surely called to become part of the answer to the psalmist's prayer—that each tender new vine may truly be cherished and protected against all that afflicts the human vineyard.

Isaiah 5:1–7
Psalm 80
Philippians 4:6–9
Matthew 21:33–43

# OCTOBER 3

*"Which of these three, in your opinion, was neighbor to the robbers' victim?" He answered, "The one who treated him with mercy." Jesus said to him, "Go and do likewise."*

—LUKE 10:36–37

May pity speak louder than blame,
Compassion louder than criticism,
Love louder than condemnation,
For this is the way of the Lord.

Jonah 1:1—2:1, 11
Jonah 2
Luke 10:25–37

*Tuesday*

# OCTOBER 4

• ST. FRANCIS OF ASSISI, RELIGIOUS •

*The Lord said to her in reply, "Martha, Martha, you are anxious and worried about many things. There is need of only one thing. Mary has chosen the better part and it will not be taken from her."*

—LUKE 10:41–42

Sometimes the good is the enemy of the better. In choosing the better, we may have to relinquish something of the merely good. May we have the grace to distinguish the better from the good and the best from the better.

Jonah 3:1–10
Psalm 130
Luke 10:38–42

*Then the LORD said, "You are concerned over the plant which cost you no labor and which you did not raise; it came up in one night and in one night it perished. And should I not be concerned over Nineveh, the great city, in which there are more than a hundred and twenty thousand persons who cannot distinguish their right hand from their left, not to mention the many cattle?"*

—JONAH 4:10–11

Nineveh is in the middle of modern Iraq. How might God be feeling now about the sorrow and confusion of the people of Nineveh?

Jonah 4:1–11
Psalm 86
Luke 11:1–4

*Ask and you will receive; seek and you will find; knock and the door will be opened to you.*

—LUKE 11:9

God's response seems not to be found in neatly packaged answers but in the slow-growing fruit of a lifetime's searching.

Malachi 3:13–20
Psalm 1
Luke 11:5–13

*Friday*

# OCTOBER 7

• OUR LADY OF THE ROSARY •

*Whoever is not with me is against me, and whoever does not gather with me scatters.*

—LUKE 11:23

I can either engage, heart and soul, with the values of the kingdom, or I can become part of the deadweight inertia that holds it back. Will I throw myself into God's justice journey or live my life like a cyclist who rides with the brakes on?

Joel 1:13–15, 2:1–2
Psalm 9
Luke 11:15–26

*While he was speaking, a woman from the crowd called out and said to him, "Blessed is the womb that carried you and the breasts at which you nursed." He replied, "Rather, blessed are those who hear the word of God and observe it."*

—LUKE 11:27–28

Jesus is looking for followers, not worshippers, for those who will walk forward with him, not look backward.

Joel 4:12–21
Psalm 97
Luke 11:27–28

*Sunday*

# OCTOBER 9

*I know indeed how to live in humble circumstances; I know also how to live with abundance. . . . I can do all things in him who strengthens me.*

—PHILIPPIANS 4:12–13

These words from Paul contrast rather drastically with the ethos of our Western consumer society, which might rewrite them like this: "I will do anything to avoid being poor and make every effort to become rich. I can master anything at all, and all in my own strength."

Will we have the courage to try Paul's way, now that our own ways have proved so disastrous?

Isaiah 25:6–10
Psalm 23
Philippians 4:12–14, 19–20
Matthew 22:1–14 or 22:1–10

*This generation is an evil generation; it seeks a sign, but no sign will be given it, except the sign of Jonah.*

—LUKE 11:29

Jonah came to grief because he kept running away from the very place he needed to be and the very business he needed to attend to. How often do I keep running, away from the situations that will never be resolved until I finally dare attend to them? The sign of Jonah—an uncomfortable sign indeed.

Romans 1:1–7
Psalm 98
Luke 11:29–32

# OCTOBER 11

*The heavens declare the glory of God,*
*and the firmament proclaims his handiwork.*
*Day pours out the word to day,*
*and night to night imparts knowledge.*

—PSALM 19:2–3

The silence of the stars is more eloquent than all our daylight clamor, the voiceless arrival of a new dawn more pregnant with meaning and promise than all our learning.

Romans 1:16–25
Psalm 19
Luke 11:37–41

# OCTOBER 12

*Only in God is my soul at rest;*
*from him comes my salvation.*
—PSALM 62:2

Day by day, night after night, in ceaseless activity and restless sleep, my life ticks on. But just occasionally the pendulum of my heart finds a timeless moment of perfect rest, in peace and prayer.

Romans 2:1–11
Psalm 62
Luke 11:42–46

*Woe to you, scholars of the law! You have taken away the key of knowledge. You yourselves did not enter and you stopped those trying to enter.*

—LUKE 11:52

The message of Christ can be locked away in a box of rules. Sometimes we stifle the very thing we most desire, and we place it out of reach, not only our reach but also that of others.

Romans 3:21–30
Psalm 130
Luke 11:47–54

*Even the hairs of your head have all been counted. Do not be afraid.*
*You are worth more than many sparrows.*

—LUKE 12:7

What new parent has not counted those tiny toes and fingers, caressed the miniature eyebrows and eyelashes, and stroked the silky little head?

Just a little bit of God's infinite love, shining through in ours.

Romans 4:1–8
Psalm 32
Luke 12:1–7

*Saturday*

# OCTOBER 15

• ST. TERESA OF JESUS, VIRGIN AND DOCTOR OF THE CHURCH •

*When they take you before synagogues and before rulers and authorities, do not worry about how or what your defense will be or about what you are to say. For the Holy Spirit will teach you at that moment what you should say.*

—LUKE 12:11–12

The wisest words are spoken when we have lost our own scripts and have to rely on God's.

Romans 4:13, 16–18
Psalm 105
Luke 12:8–12

*Repay to Caesar what belongs to Caesar and to God what belongs to God.*

—MATTHEW 22:21

Caesar's are the armies and the banks and the multinational corporations.

God's are the daisies and the sparrows that will still be here when all our empires fade.

Isaiah 45:1, 4–6
Psalm 96
1 Thessalonians 1:1–5
Matthew 22:15–21

*Take care to guard against all greed, for though one may be rich, one's life does not consist of possessions.*

—LUKE 12:15

We enter life and leave it owning nothing, and a blip on the stock market, a single wrong decision, or an unpredictable accident can wipe out what we think we own in the intervening years. The bedrock of God's love can feel like an illusion, but it turns out to be the only solid truth.

Romans 4:20–25
Luke 1:69–75
Luke 12:13–21

# OCTOBER 18

• ST. LUKE, EVANGELIST •

*After this the Lord Jesus appointed seventy-two disciples whom he sent
ahead of him in pairs to every town and place he intended to visit. He
said to them, "The harvest is abundant but the laborers are few; so ask
the master of the harvest to send out laborers for his harvest. Go on
your way; behold, I am sending you like lambs among wolves."*

—LUKE 10:1–3

In the northern steppes, the wolves rule the winter season,
making the high plateau their own. In the pastures, the
lambs herald the coming of spring. Both will be close by
along our journey, but perhaps today Jesus is reminding us
that however harsh the winter of our lives may be, the new
life of springtime will always prevail.

2 Timothy 4:10–17
Psalm 145
Luke 10:1–9

*We were rescued like a bird*
*from the flowler's snare,*
*Broken was the snare,*
*and we were freed.*
—PSALM 124:7

There are birds that, when their legs become trapped in a snare, tear off their own limbs to get free. Genuine freedom is always worth the pain it may cost.

Romans 6:12–18
Psalm 124
Luke 12:39–48

# OCTOBER 20

*I have come to set the earth on fire, and how I wish it were
already blazing!*

—LUKE 12:49

The fire that Jesus brings is like the fire that bursts open
the eucalyptus seeds in the stricken Australian outback and
enables new life. It is a refiner's fire that feels like the end of
life as we know it but is actually the beginning of life as we
have yet to discover it.

Romans 6:19–23
Psalm 1
Luke 12:49–53

*You know how to interpret the appearance of the earth and the sky; why do you not know how to interpret the present time?*

—LUKE 12:56

Before the Asian tsunami in 2004, the ants and the elephants and many other creatures sensed the danger and moved inland. Only humankind missed the signals. Could it be that our superior intellect has smothered deeper intuitive powers? Have we bought knowledge at the cost of wisdom?

Romans 7:18–25
Psalm 119
Luke 12:54–59

*Who can ascend the mountain of the LORD?*
*or who may stand in his holy place?*
*He whose hands are sinless, whose heart is clean,*
*who desires not what is vain.*

—PSALM 24:3–4

Pioneers must travel light. The clutter of worthless things
will make our journey to the holy place of God's unfolding
impossible. What must we leave behind in our pilgrimage
to the mountain of the Lord?

Romans 8:1–11
Psalm 24
Luke 13:1–9

———————————

*You shall not wrong any widow or orphan. If ever you wrong them
and they cry out to me, I will surely hear their cry.*

—EXODUS 22:21–22

What we say on our lips becomes much harder if we really
practice it in our lives or seek to integrate it in our national
policies and social systems. Yet the cries of the poor are
not silenced, and they never fail to reach the ear of God.

Exodus 22:20–26
Psalm 18
1 Thessalonians 1:5–10
Matthew 22:34–40

# OCTOBER 24

*You did not receive a spirit of slavery to fall back into fear, but you received a spirit of adoption, through which we cry, "Abba, Father!"*
—ROMANS 8:15

Slaves have no say in what happens to them, no role in helping to shape the future.

Slaves are not consulted or respected. Their labor is taken and used but not rewarded.

Have we really abolished slavery?

None of us can claim to be a son or daughter of the Father until all of us are free.

Romans 8:12–17
Psalm 68
Luke 13:10–17

# OCTOBER 25

*We know that all creation is groaning in labor pains even until now.*
—ROMANS 8:22

Giving birth always involves pain. It always involves a leaving behind of the comfort zone to enter a wholly new dimension of life.

We are all called to be midwives in the birthing of God's dream on this planet.

Romans 8:18–25
Psalm 126
Luke 13:18–21

*We do not know how to pray as we ought, but the Spirit himself
intercedes with inexpressible groanings. And the one who searches hearts
knows what is the intention of the Spirit, because it intercedes for the
holy ones according to God's will.*

—ROMANS 8:26–27

There are times when the deepest longings of our hearts
lie beyond words, and silence is the only possible channel
of communication. Unhampered by our words, God's
Spirit can then flow more perfectly than we can guess
or imagine.

Romans 8:26–30
Psalm 13
Luke 13:22–30

*For I am convinced that neither death, nor life, nor angels, nor principalities, nor present things, nor future things, nor powers, nor height, nor depth, nor any other creature will be able to separate us from the love of God in Christ Jesus our Lord.*

—ROMANS 8:38–39

Nothing can stop the power of the sun from energizing our life on earth, however many clouds intervene.

Nothing can block the love of God from energizing our innermost being, whatever anxieties or crises engage our conscious minds.

Romans 8:31–39
Psalm 109
Luke 13:31–35

*You are fellow citizens with the holy ones and members of the household of God, built upon the foundation of the Apostles and prophets, with Christ Jesus himself as the capstone. Through him the whole structure is held together and grows into a temple sacred in the Lord.*

—EPHESIANS 2:19–21

And yet it is the responsibility of every brick, from the rooftop to the basement, to keep on asking, "Am I truly aligned to the cornerstone?" The holiness and the wholeness of the temple depend on it.

Ephesians 2:19–22
Psalm 19
Luke 6:12–16

# OCTOBER 29

*The gifts and the call of God are irrevocable.*

—ROMANS 11:29

When our confidence flounders and our self-respect goes
into free fall, let us remember that it is we, not God, who
have lost faith in ourselves.

Romans 11:1–2, 11–12, 25–29
Psalm 94
Luke 14:1, 7–11

*I have stilled and quieted
my soul like a weaned child.
Like a weaned child on its mother's lap,
so is my soul within me.*

—PSALM 131:2

When I hold my baby granddaughter in my arms, I marvel at her absolute trust in me not to drop her or fail her. If she can place such trust in me, how much more can I trust the One in whom I live and move and have my being?

Malachi 1:14—2:2, 8–10
Psalm 131
1 Thessalonians 2:7–9, 13
Matthew 23:1–12

*When you hold a banquet, invite the poor, the crippled, the lame, the blind; blessed indeed will you be because of their inability to repay you. For you will be repaid at the resurrection of the righteous.*

—LUKE 14:13–14

In a culture where everything carries a price tag, it is especially hard to get free of the payback mentality and love for the sake of simply loving. These words of Jesus' could occupy us for a lifetime and still leave us deeply disturbed.

Romans 11:29–36
Psalm 69
Luke 14:12–14

*Beloved, we are God's children now; what we shall be has not yet been revealed. We do know that when it is revealed we shall be like him, for we shall see him as he is.*

—1 JOHN 3:2

A silversmith holds a piece of silver ore in the heat of the fire for as long as it takes for the pure silver to be revealed. "How do you know when it has been completely purified?" asks an interested bystander. "That's easy," replies the silversmith. "When the purification is complete I can see my image in it."

Revelation 7:2–4, 9–14
Psalm 24
1 John 3:1–3
Matthew 5:1–12

*Wednesday*

# NOVEMBER 2

*Everything that the Father gives me will come to me, and I will not reject anyone who comes to me.*

—JOHN 6:37

When those we love travel beyond our mortal horizon, what joy to know that they are journeying home to the One who will not turn them away. What reassurance to realize that all endings are new beginnings and that what seems like loss will become amazing rediscovery in a dimension far beyond our human understanding.

Wisdom 3:1–9
Psalm 27
Romans 5:5–11 or 6:3–9
John 6:37–40
or other readings

*None of us lives for oneself, and no one dies for oneself. For if we live, we live for the Lord, and if we die, we die for the Lord; so then, whether we live or die, we are the Lord's.*

—ROMANS 14:7–8

Every subatomic particle is interrelated with and interdependent on every other. What is true for subatomic particles is magnified a millionfold when it comes to human beings.

Romans 14:7–12
Psalm 27
Luke 15:1–10

*For the children of this world are more prudent in dealing with their own generation than are the children of light.*

—LUKE 16:8

Faith is not about naïveté but about having the strength and courage to apply the values of Jesus to the very complex and challenging issues of life as we are really living it. Faith is a matter of walking a fine and balanced line between idealism and pragmatism.

Romans 15:14–21
Psalm 98
Luke 16:1–8

# NOVEMBER 5

*The person who is trustworthy in very small matters is also
trustworthy in great ones; and the person who is dishonest in very
small matters is also dishonest in great ones. If, therefore, you are not
trustworthy with dishonest wealth, who will trust you with true wealth?*

—LUKE 16:10–11

If I can trust you with my dreams, I don't need to wonder
whether I can trust you with my dollars.

Romans 16:3–9, 16, 22–27
Psalm 145
Luke 16:9–15

# NOVEMBER 6

*The kingdom of heaven will be like ten virgins who took their lamps and went out to meet the bridegroom. Five of them were foolish and five were wise. The foolish ones, when taking their lamps, brought no oil with them, but the wise brought flasks of oil with their lamps.*

—MATTHEW 25:1–4

So many of us begin with a surge of prayer and a burst of enthusiasm, but the energy for the long haul runs out and leaves us in the dark. The wise bridesmaids show us what to do about that.

Wisdom 6:12–16
Psalm 63
1 Thessalonians 4:13–18 or 4:13–14
Matthew 25:1–13

———

*If I take the wings of the dawn,*
*if I settle at the farthest limits of the sea,*
*Even there your hand shall guide me,*
*and your right hand hold me fast.*

—PSALM 139:9–10

Every journey we make, however far reaching, is a circular
tour, bringing us back to the God who dwells within us,
right where we began.

Wisdom 1:1–7
Psalm 139
Luke 17:1–6

*God formed man to be imperishable;*
*the image of his own nature he made him.*

—WISDOM 2:23

We will discover the imperishable center of who we really
are when life has stripped away all the outer, perishable
layers that have accumulated around us.

Wisdom 2:23—3:9
Psalm 34
Luke 17:7–10

*He made a whip out of cords and drove them all out of the temple area,
with the sheep and oxen, and spilled the coins of the money-changers
and overturned their tables, and to those who sold doves he said, "Take
these out of here, and stop making my Father's house a marketplace."*

—JOHN 2:15–16

The warning still holds true today: the worship of God
is not compatible with the self-focused pursuit of profit
and power.

Ezekiel 47:1–2, 8–9, 12
Psalm 46
1 Corinthians 3:9–11, 16–17
John 2:13–22

*Indeed, [Wisdom] reaches from end to end mightily
and governs all things well.*

—WISDOM 8:1

Perhaps this is the bottom line of faith: to trust that divine wisdom holds all things in goodness, truth, and loving power and that no harm can ultimately subvert it.

Wisdom 7:22—8:1
Psalm 119
Luke 17:20–25

*For all men were by nature foolish who were in ignorance of God,*
*and who from the good things seen did not succeed in knowing him*
*who is,*
*and from studying the works did not discern the artisan.*

—WISDOM 13:1

How easy it is to eat the bread and fail to notice the
baker, to dance to the music but ignore the composer, to
gaze at the signpost but miss the destination to which it
points. I guess the writer of Wisdom wouldn't give us very
high grades!

Wisdom 13:1–9
Psalm 19
Luke 17:26–37

• ST. JOSAPHAT, BISHOP AND MARTYR •

*For when peaceful stillness compassed everything
and the night in its swift course was half spent,
Your all-powerful word from heaven's royal throne
bounded, a fierce warrior, into the doomed land.*

—WISDOM 18:14–15

The Word leaps into our lives halfway through the story,
making sense of all that has been and empowering us for all
that shall become.

Wisdom 18:14–16; 19:6–9
Psalm 105
Luke 18:1–8

# NOVEMBER 13

*To everyone who has, more will be given and he will grow rich; but
from the one who has not, even what he has will be taken away.*

—MATTHEW 25:29

Grace has a habit of multiplying itself when we cooperate
with it and of shrinking away from us when we ignore it.

Proverbs 31:10–13, 19–20, 30–31
Psalm 128
1 Thessalonians 5:1–6
Matthew 25:14–30 or 25:14–15, 19–21

*He shouted, "Jesus, Son of David, have pity on me!" The people
walking in front rebuked him, telling him to be silent, but he kept calling
out all the more, "Son of David, have pity on me!"*

—LUKE 18:38–39

When the pain has gone too deep and our words cannot
express our need, then our unspeakable cries rise to God
and will not be silenced.

1 Maccabees 1:10–15, 41–43, 54–57, 62–63
Psalm 119
Luke 18:35–43

*So he ran ahead and climbed a sycamore tree in order to see Jesus, who was about to pass that way. When he reached the place, Jesus looked up and said to him, "Zacchaeus, come down quickly, for today I must stay at your house." And he came down quickly and received him with joy.*

—LUKE 19:4–6

When we think that we are much too small to be noticed, when we feel safe in our hideaway, beware! That might be the very time when God stops by, looks us in the eye, and comes home for lunch.

2 Maccabees 6:18–31
Psalm 3
Luke 19:1–10

# NOVEMBER 16

*Hide me in the shadow of your wings.*
*But I in justice shall behold your face;*
*on waking, I shall be content in your presence.*
—PSALM 17:8, 15

Jody was in despair. When night fell all she could do
was sink into God's presence and bury herself in God's
compassion. The morning brought new hope, new vision,
and the possibility of a new beginning.

2 Maccabees 7:1, 20–31
Psalm 17
Luke 19:11–28

*As Jesus drew near Jerusalem, he saw the city and wept over it, saying,*
*"If this day you only knew what makes for peace—but now it is hidden*
*from your eyes."*

—LUKE 19:41–42

The time to understand the message of peace is the
moment before we launch the preemptive strike. After we
have acted, the opportunity for new directions will have
passed and may remain hidden from our eyes forever.

1 Maccabees 2:15–29
Psalm 50
Luke 19:41–44

*It is written, "My house shall be a house of prayer, but you have made it a den of thieves."*

—LUKE 19:46

When prophets turn to profits, we have lost our way.

1 Maccabees 4:36–37, 52–59
1 Chronicles 29:10–12
Luke 19:45–48

*The nations are sunk in the pit they have made;*
*in the snare they set, their foot is caught.*
*For the needy shall not always be forgotten,*
*nor shall the hope of the afflicted forever perish.*

—PSALM 9:16, 19

As the Communist regimes in Eastern Europe began
to crumble, the men and women who had long been
oppressed proclaimed, "You call this a 'people's republic'
but we are the people!"

From that point on, the dictatorships were caught by their
own rhetoric, and the voice of the poor prevailed.

1 Maccabees 6:1–13
Psalm 9
Luke 20:27–40

# NOVEMBER 20

*The lost I will seek out, the strayed I will bring back, the injured I will bind up, the sick I will heal, but the sleek and the strong I will destroy, shepherding them rightly.*

—EZEKIEL 34:16

When I see police and social workers tirelessly searching for a missing child, when I see medics fighting to save lives and ordinary people attending quietly to the troubles of their neighbors, then I know the true Shepherd is the source of their goodness.

Ezekiel 34:11–12, 15–17
Psalm 23
1 Corinthians 15:20–26, 28
Matthew 25:31–46

*He said, "I tell you truly, this poor widow put in more than all the rest;*
*for those others have all made offerings from their surplus wealth, but*
*she, from her poverty, has offered her whole livelihood."*

—LUKE 21:3–4

To give away our spare cash may be an act of charity, but
to give away what we need for the next meal is an act of
radical trust. At those times, we prove our faith that the
One who made us will sustain us just as we seek to sustain
one another.

Daniel 1:1–6, 8–20
Daniel 3:52–56
Luke 21:1–4

*Then he said to them, "Nation will rise against nation, and kingdom against kingdom. There will be powerful earthquakes, famines, and plagues from place to place; and awesome sights and mighty signs will come from the sky."*

—LUKE 21:10–11

Whenever something new is coming to birth, there will always be great pain, fear, and turmoil. Perhaps even now, in these times, we are thrashing in our labor pains. Can we trust the divine midwife to turn our travail into new life?

Daniel 2:31–45
Daniel 3:57–61
Luke 21:5–11

# NOVEMBER 23

*Remember, you are not to prepare your defense beforehand, for I myself shall give you a wisdom in speaking that all your adversaries will be powerless to resist or refute.*

—LUKE 21:14–15

When words fail us, our deepest passions may find unexpected expression in words not our own. At those times, we will ignite the hearts of those who hear us with the very spirit of God.

Daniel 5:1–6, 13–14, 16–17, 23–28
Daniel 3:62–67
Luke 21:12–19

# NOVEMBER 24

*Woe to pregnant women and nursing mothers in those days, for a terrible calamity will come upon the earth and a wrathful judgment upon this people.*

—LUKE 21:23

A slip of paper, placed beside the body of a dead child in Ravensbrück concentration camp reads: "Do not remember all the suffering they have inflicted on us—remember instead the fruits we have bought, thanks to this suffering: our comradeship, our loyalty, our humility, our courage, our generosity, the greatness of heart which has grown out of all this. . . . When those who have inflicted suffering on us come to judgment, let all the fruits which we have borne be their forgiveness."

Daniel 6:12–28
Daniel 3:68–74
Luke 21:20–28

# NOVEMBER 25

*Consider the fig tree and all the other trees. When their buds burst open, you see for yourselves and know that summer is now near; in the same way, when you see these things happening, know that the Kingdom of God is near.*

—LUKE 21:29–31

It can take a brushfire to burst open the eucalyptus seed, to liberate new life. Perhaps it shouldn't surprise us that the seeds of God's kingdom may burst free in the fire of frightening change and transition.

Daniel 7:2–14
Daniel 3:75–81
Luke 21:29–33

# NOVEMBER 26

*Be vigilant at all times and pray that you have the strength to escape the tribulations that are imminent and to stand before the Son of Man.*

—LUKE 21:36

The captain of a ship, facing a storm, will strive to stay perfectly focused on holding the vessel steady. He finds the strength to keep going in calm alertness to the present moment.

Daniel 7:15–27
Daniel 3:82–87
Luke 21:34–36

*No ear has ever heard, no eye ever seen, any God but you
doing such deeds for those who wait for him.*

—ISAIAH 64:3

As a new year approaches, may we, like newborn babes
in a new place, open our eyes and ears, as if for the first
time. May we greet with open hearts the good news that is
coming to pass.

Isaiah 63:16–17, 19; 64:2–7
Psalm 80
1 Corinthians 1:3–9
Mark 13:33–37

# NOVEMBER 28

*In days to come,*
*The mountain of the LORD's house*
*shall be established as the highest mountain*
*... All nations shall stream toward it;*
*many peoples shall come and say:*
*"Come, let us climb the LORD's mountain,*
*to the house of the God of Jacob,*
*That he may instruct us in his ways,*
*and we may walk in his paths."*

—ISAIAH 2:2–3

Perhaps the mountain has a name: the moral high ground.
No nation has the right to claim it, but the One who is
coming makes a home there and will draw all of us closer
to its sacred slopes.

Isaiah 2:1–5
Psalm 122
Matthew 8:5–11

# NOVEMBER 29

*A shoot shall sprout from the stump of Jesse,*
*and from his roots a bud shall blossom.*
*The Spirit of the LORD shall rest upon him:*
*a Spirit of wisdom and of understanding,*
*A Spirit of counsel and of strength,*
*a Spirit of knowledge and of fear of the LORD.*

—ISAIAH 11:1–2

This is no hesitant spirit, no shy retiring violet, but a surge of life-transforming grace pushing out from the ancient root of our sacred story. This spirit will bear new fruit, new ways of thinking and relating, a fresh wind in the universe.

Isaiah 11:1–10
Psalm 72
Luke 10:21–24

# NOVEMBER 30

• ST. ANDREW, APOSTLE •

*As Jesus was walking by the Sea of Galilee, he saw two brothers,*
*Simon who is called Peter, and his brother Andrew, casting a net into*
*the sea; they were fishermen. He said to them, "Come after me, and I will*
*make you fishers of men."*

—MATTHEW 4:18–19

I wandered along the beach in northeastern Scotland,
where my family has its roots, and listened to the local
fishermen talking to one another in their broad dialect.
These were men toughened by a hard life at sea, men who
knew what life is truly about. I imagined what they would
have made of Jesus' call and marveled at the magnetic
power of this man who can attract instant allegiance, even
across thousands of years, from the toughest and most
skeptical hearts.

Romans 10:9–18
Psalm 19
Matthew 4:18–22

# DECEMBER 1

*Open to me the gates of justice;*
*I will enter them and give thanks to the LORD.*

—PSALM 118:19

It always takes me by surprise that when the gates of
holiness open, however briefly, they usually reveal not
some distant castle in the sky but our own backyard. Holy
gates invite us to discover God right here.

Isaiah 26:1–6
Psalm 118
Matthew 7:21, 24–27

*The LORD is my light and my salvation;*
*whom should I fear?*
*The LORD is my life's refuge;*
*of whom should I be afraid?*
—PSALM 27:1

When I walk in God's light, I don't need to fear whatever
may be lurking in the darkness.

When I lean back on God, I don't need to fear whatever
may be standing in front of me.

Isaiah 29:17–24
Psalm 27
Matthew 9:27–31

*Without cost you have received; without cost you are to give.*

—MATTHEW 10:8

We come into this world with nothing but God's abundant gifts. All we can add to them is our own price tag. Doesn't that bring up some questions about the honesty of our accounting?

Isaiah 30:19–21, 23–26
Psalm 147
Matthew 9:35—10:1, 5a, 6–8

# DECEMBER 4

• SECOND SUNDAY OF ADVENT •

*Make straight in the wasteland a highway for our God!*
*Every valley shall be filled in,*
*every mountain and hill shall be made low;*
*The rugged land shall be made a plain,*
*the rough country, a broad valley.*

—ISAIAH 40:3–4

God is the great leveler. This work may involve much more than smoothing out the mountains of difficulty and the valleys of despair. It may also mean leveling down the mountains of all-consuming prosperity to fill the gaping emptiness in the valleys of poverty.

Isaiah 40:1–5, 9–11
Psalm 85
2 Peter 3:8–14
Mark 1:1–8

*Strengthen the hands that are feeble,*
*make firm the knees that are weak,*
*Say to those whose hearts are frightened:*
*Be strong, fear not!*
—ISAIAH 35:3–4

The irony is that we cannot hear these encouraging words
and take them to heart until our hands are weary, our
knees are trembling, and our hearts are faint. Only then do
we understand the power and love behind those actions.

Isaiah 35:1–10
Psalm 85
Luke 5:17–26

# DECEMBER 6

*What is your opinion? If a man has a hundred sheep and one of them goes astray, will he not leave the ninety-nine in the hills and go in search of the stray?*

—MATTHEW 18:12

The television news broadcasts an appeal for a missing child. The local police force, the entire neighborhood, and all the friends and family are out searching. Those who love the little one will search ceaselessly for as long as it takes, for a lifetime if necessary. If we care that much, what can we say about God?

Isaiah 40:1–11
Psalm 96
Matthew 18:12–14

*He does not faint nor grow weary,*
*and his knowledge is beyond scrutiny.*
*He gives strength to the fainting;*
*for the weak he makes vigor abound.*
—ISAIAH 40:28–29

The One with unlimited understanding and boundless energy wants nothing more than to give it away to us, who have nothing.

Isaiah 40:25–31
Psalm 103
Matthew 11:28–30

⋟ 375 ⋞

• THE IMMACULATE CONCEPTION OF THE BLESSED VIRGIN MARY •

*Mary said, "Behold, I am the handmaid of the Lord. May it be done to me according to your word."*

—LUKE 1:38

When the Spirit hovers over our hearts, we have two choices: to resist and close down or to give our unconditional consent for God's dream to come to birth in our lives. There is no halfway position. It's not possible to be only a little bit pregnant.

Genesis 3:9–15, 20
Psalm 98
Ephesians 1:3–6, 11–12
Luke 1:26–38

*If you would hearken to my commandments,*
*your prosperity would be like a river,*
*and your vindication like the waves of the sea.*

—ISAIAH 48:18

It's important to remember what might have been, but only
as an aid in learning from the past, so that we can make a
different kind of future.

Isaiah 48:17–19
Psalm 1
Matthew 11:16–19

# DECEMBER 10

*Blessed is he who shall have seen you
and who falls asleep in your friendship.*
—SIRACH 48:11

Does that seem to rule you and me out of the running?
We haven't seen God—or perhaps we have: in the daily
miracles that lie everywhere around us. We haven't died
yet—perhaps we can, at the end of every day that closes
with a thankful heart and a mind at peace with those
around us.

Sirach 48:1–4, 9–11
Psalm 80
Matthew 17:9a, 10–13

≥ 378 ≤

*As the earth brings forth its plants,*
*and a garden makes its growth spring up,*
*So will the Lord* GOD *make justice and praise*
*spring up before all the nations.*

—ISAIAH 61:11

God's creation is organic, dynamic, alive, and always growing big dreams from tiny possibilities. Just as God draws the fruit and the flower from a little seed, so, too, God is drawing the very best from every person and every nation.

Isaiah 61:1–2, 10–11
Luke 1:46–50, 53–54
1 Thessalonians 5:16–24
John 1:6–8, 19–28

*[The angel] said, "Hail, full of grace! The Lord is with you." But she was greatly troubled at what was said and pondered what sort of greeting this might be. Then the angel said to her, "Do not be afraid, Mary, for you have found favor with God. Behold, you will conceive in your womb and bear a son, and you shall name him Jesus."*

—LUKE 1:28–31

Whenever God's power touches human lives, whether in dramatic visions or subtle inner movements, our natural reaction is to feel disturbed and fearful. If we dare to trust the angel's reassurance, however, our fear can be transformed into awe and our resistance into life-changing response.

Zechariah 2:14–17 or Revelation 11:19; 12:1–6, 10
Judith 13:18–19
Luke 1:26–38 or 1:39–47

*Tuesday*

# DECEMBER 13

• ST. LUCY, VIRGIN AND MARTYR •

*On that day
You need not be ashamed
of all your deeds,
your rebellious actions against me;
For then will I remove from your midst
the proud braggarts,
And you shall no longer exalt yourself
on my holy mountain.*

—ZEPHANIAH 3:11

Imagine a children's game in which the Barbie dolls and toy soldiers come alive and take over the planet. I sometimes wonder whether this is how we appear to God as we strut around on God's holy mountain, Earth.

Zephaniah 3:1–2, 9–13
Psalm 34
Matthew 21:28–32

*I am the LORD, there is no other;*
*I form the light, and create the darkness,*
*I make well-being and create woe;*
*I, the LORD, do all these things.*

—ISAIAH 45:6

We could read this comment as an expression of the illusion we have of being the center of the universe. It is the task of a lifetime to recognize this as the illusion it is and then to discover that God alone is the axis around which all creation spins.

Isaiah 45:6–8, 18, 21–25
Psalm 85
Luke 7:18–23

# DECEMBER 15

*Though the mountains leave their place*
*and the hills be shaken,*
*My love shall never leave you*
*nor my covenant of peace be shaken.*

—ISAIAH 54:10

In the devastation left behind by the most disastrous earthquake, we find human hands reaching out to feed the starving and bind the wounded. In the wake of a catastrophic tsunami, we hear the march of human feet rushing to help and to rescue. These are the hands and feet of Christ.

Will ours be among them?

Isaiah 54:1–10
Psalm 30
Luke 7:24–30

*Thus says the* LORD:
*Observe what is right, do what is just;*
*for my salvation is about to come,*
*my justice, about to be revealed.*

—ISAIAH 56:1

There is a causal connection here. It is those who care for justice and act with integrity who are preparing the way for the salvation we long for. And it is those whose hearts are just and whose eyes see the truth who will recognize it when it is revealed.

Isaiah 56:1–3, 6–8
Psalm 67
John 5:33–36

*The mountains shall yield peace for the people,*
*and the hills justice.*

—PSALM 72:3

All creation is striving to bring forth a mystery beyond itself, a kingdom of peace and justice. The created world models it, the prophets foretell it, the psalmist celebrates it, and Jesus shows us what it looks like in reality. All of these invite us to let God's kingdom come to birth in our own lives.

Genesis 49:2, 8–10
Psalm 72
Matthew 1:1–17

# DECEMBER 18

*The angel said to her in reply, "The Holy Spirit will come upon you,*
*and the power of the Most High will overshadow you."*

—LUKE 1:35

The mere shadow of God is brighter than our brightest
sunlight, and it rests upon us with a generative, life-giving
power that bursts open our imagination and potential.

2 Samuel 7:1–5, 8–12, 14, 16
Psalm 89
Romans 16:25–27
Luke 1:26–38

# DECEMBER 19

*But now you will be speechless and unable to talk until the day these things take place, because you did not believe my words, which will be fulfilled at their proper time.*

—LUKE 1:20

I pray that if I do not speak from a baseline of faith and trust, I, too, might be silenced, or at the very least that others might have the good sense not to listen to me.

Judges 13:2–7, 24–25
Psalm 71
Luke 1:5–25

# DECEMBER 20

*They will receive blessings from the LORD,*
*and justice from their saving God.*
*Such are the people that love the LORD,*
*that seek the face of the God of Jacob.*

—PSALM 24: 5–6

Do we dare offer God the blank check of our hearts and souls and lives? Can we do this—will we do it—knowing that it may cost us all we have and all we are?

Isaiah 7:10–14
Psalm 24
Luke 1:26–38

# DECEMBER 21

• ST. PETER CANISIUS, PRIEST AND DOCTOR OF THE CHURCH •

*Blessed are you who believed that what was spoken to you by the Lord would be fulfilled.*

—LUKE 1:45

God's promises are like seeds. If they take root in our hearts, if we really trust them, then they will grow to fulfillment and bear the fruits of blessing for ourselves and for others.

Song of Songs 2:8–14 or Zephaniah 3:14–18
Psalm 33
Luke 1:39–45

*I prayed for this child, and the LORD granted my request. Now I, in turn, give him to the LORD; as long as he lives, he shall be dedicated to the LORD.*

—1 SAMUEL 1:27–28

When a gift we have longed for and that truly comes from God is actually given to us, then a strange thing happens. We lose any desire to keep it all to ourselves and experience instead a desire to give it back to God, to be multiplied and shared among many.

1 Samuel 1:24–28
1 Samuel 2:1, 4–8
Luke 1:46–56

*All who heard these things took them to heart, saying, "What, then, will this child be?" For surely the hand of the Lord was with him.*

—LUKE 1:66

Whenever we gaze at a newborn baby we might ask, "What fragment of God's dream will this new life reveal?" The newborn John was to become the pointer to the One who would reveal all of it.

Malachi 3:1–4, 23–24
Psalm 25
Luke 1:57–66

# DECEMBER 24

*You, my child, shall be called prophet of the Most High,*
*for you will go before the Lord to prepare his way,*
*to give his people knowledge of salvation*
*through the forgiveness of their sins.*

—LUKE 1: 76–77

We stand, tonight, on the threshold of the new covenant. Leadership now rests in the hands of a little child who comes, helpless, humble, and poor, to prepare human hearts and minds for a new vision of God's dream for God's people. This little child will turn all our assumptions on their heads. Will we recognize him? Will we have the courage to follow where he leads?

2 Samuel 7:1–5, 8–12, 14, 16
Psalm 89
Luke 1:67–79

# DECEMBER 25

• THE NATIVITY OF THE LORD • CHRISTMAS •

*What came to be through him was life,*
*and this life was the light of the human race;*
*the light shines in the darkness,*
*and the darkness has not overcome it.*

—JOHN 1:3–5

A first-century philosopher observed: "When I light a candle at midnight, I say to the darkness: 'I beg to differ.'" As we light our Christmas candles, we, too, say to the darkness in our world and in our own hearts, "You have no final power over us, for the first and final word is eternal light."

**Vigil:**
Isaiah 62:1–5
Psalm 89
Acts 13:16–17, 22–25
Matthew 1:1–25 or 1:18–25

**Midnight:**
Isaiah 9:1–6
Psalm 96
Titus 2:11–14
Luke 2:1–14

**Dawn:**
Isaiah 62:11–12
Psalm 97
Titus 3:4–7
Luke 2:15–20

**Day:**
Isaiah 52:7–10
Psalm 98
Hebrews 1:1–6
John 1:1–18 or 1:1–5, 9–14

*But he, filled with the Holy Spirit, looked up intently to heaven and saw the glory of God and Jesus standing at the right hand of God, and he said, "Behold, I see the heavens opened and the Son of Man standing at the right hand of God."*

—ACTS 7:55–56

The stones that battered Stephen's body broke open the doorways of his soul to reveal to him the eternal promise of God, transcending the very worst that human cruelty can inflict.

Acts 6:8–10, 7:54–59
Psalm 31
Matthew 10:17–22

*For the life was made visible;*
*we have seen it and testify to it*
*and proclaim to you the eternal life*
*that was with the Father and was made visible to us.*

—1 JOHN 1:2

A little girl discovered her granny spinning golden thread in the midst of a dark and dangerous forest. As a token of her love, Granny tied one end of the thread to the child's finger and sent her back to the forest with the promise: "Wherever you go, whatever happens, you are connected to me by this golden thread, which can never be broken." Jesus is to us the visible evidence of God's continuous presence and love.

1 John 1:1–4
Psalm 97
John 20:1a, 2–8

# DECEMBER 28

• THE HOLY INNOCENTS, MARTYRS •

*This is the message that we have heard from Jesus Christ and proclaim
to you: God is light, and in him there is no darkness at all. If we say,
"We have fellowship with him," while we continue to walk in darkness,
we lie and do not act in truth.*

—1 JOHN 1:5–6

It takes only one candle to banish the darkness from the
darkest of rooms. It takes only one gleam of faith to banish
the fear from the darkest of situations.

It may be asked of each and any of us, at any time, to light
that single candle in our own situations. In the midst of the
pain, fright, or confusion, we may be the only ones who
have a candle or the faith to light it.

1 John 1:5—2:2
Psalm 124
Matthew 2:13–18

*Simeon blessed them and said to Mary his mother, "Behold, this child is destined for the fall and rise of many in Israel, and to be a sign that will be contradicted (and you yourself a sword will pierce) so that the thoughts of many hearts may be revealed."*

—LUKE 2:34–35

I love to think of Jesus having godparents. Today we meet Simeon, whom I like to think of as a godfather to this very special child. His insight penetrates the mystery that he's witnessing. He sees both falling and rising, death and new birth, something wonderfully offered and incredibly rejected. He sees a blade of truth and integrity that will both wound and heal.

1 John 2:3–11
Psalm 96
Luke 2:22–35

*Friday*

# DECEMBER 30

• THE HOLY FAMILY OF JESUS, MARY, AND JOSEPH •

*When they had fulfilled all the prescriptions of the law of the Lord, they returned to Galilee, to their own town of Nazareth. The child grew and became strong, filled with wisdom, and the favor of God was upon him.*

—LUKE 2:39–40

The pattern set by the Holy Family holds good for all families in every culture and every age. First, discipline provides the foundation for healthy growth, and growth allows wisdom to emerge, and God's blessing and favor embraces the whole process.

Sirach 3:2–7, 12–14 or Colossians 3:12–21 or 3:12–17
Psalm 128
Luke 2:22–40 or 2:22, 39–40

⋟ 398 ⋞